This book will change your life for the better. TODAY.

Brad Burton is back, sharing his unique and raw look at life/business and how everything happens for a reason, even the shitty stuff.

BRAD BURTON

4PUBLISHING

WWW.4PUBLISHING.BIZ

First published in 2011 by 4Publishing
2 The Crescent, Taunton, Somerset, TA1 4EA, United Kingdom

hello@4publishing.biz
www.4publishing.biz

4Publishing is a trading style of 4Networking Ltd

ISBN 978-1-907451-02-7

Dedicated to

The People's Pash. Sarah.

Wifey's Dad. Ray of Sunshine.

BRAD

Get Off Your Arse and do something. Anything. TODAY.

GOYA is not just the title of my first book, it's a rousing call to action. As a result, since *GOYA* was first published in 2009, the response has been incredible:

- Over 100 5★ reviews on Amazon: *GOYA* averages 4.9 out of 5!

- Brad Burton touring the country and delivering the *GOYA* message to packed audiences at networking events, exhibitions and seminars.

- Brad's profile rising steadily in the media, with appearances on the BBC's *Working Lunch* and Radio 2, in national newspapers and in the business press.

Read reviews on Amazon and on the *GOYA* site (+ add your own!) Here's a small selection:

It is truly THE most inspirational read I have EVER read and as a coach I have read lots of material.
Scott Dwyer, Motivations Business Coaching Services

There were parts of the book that made me laugh out loud, others that made me shout "that's so true" and others that brought a lump to my throat. This was definitely the best book I read in the whole of 2009.
Danielle Fagot, Richmond House

"Aggressively waiting for the phone to ring": that phrase will haunt me for the rest of my business life – it made me feel like a school kid who had been caught smoking or something, gave me the kick up the ass I deserved. In case I haven't mentioned it Brad – THANKS!
Rob Wilkinson, Call Centre Connect

GOYA Audio Book (read by Brad!) and GOYA Kindle/iBooks

All available now from *www.getoffyourarse.biz*

Contents

Contents

Foreword

We are in a time when banks are still paying bonuses despite not having repaid the taxpayer untold billions, when central banks are resorting to just printing money, and when the state is slashing spending without developing true efficiencies. We are entering a period of significant turbulence, with no shortage of doom-mongers predicting the collapse of western currencies, pensions crises and demographic time-bombs.

If you pay heed to the doom-merchants (or negheads as Brad calls them) you will rob yourself of your own power by focussing on covering your arse rather than getting off it. This is where this book comes in, for it shows you with understanding and compassion how powerful getting off your arse can be...

Brad has come from the backstreets of Salford, with limited formal education, some significant challenges on the way, long periods of unemployment and therefore in a perfect place to play the blame game. But is that what he did? Far from it: he tried to play the 'right' game of climbing up the corporate ladder and realised, despite his award winning success, that the dice were stacked against him. So he decided to take control of the dice and roll his own. A long and painful journey of education and insight followed, which he now shares in this illuminating book, for he not only shows you the way but also provides a set of tools and support, available from his own network, 4Networking.

Brad and I met by chance in late 2005 as exhibitors at a 'business' (more like craft) fair in Bridgwater town hall in sleepy Somerset. Although polar opposites in many ways, we hit it off, creating more as a team than we did individually, and as a result 4Networking was born a few short months later. In many ways *GOYA Too* should be the first book in the series as it shows the 'why' and the 'way' of *GOYA*. Like sliding gently into a hot bath, this books sets you up perfectly to read or re-visit the first *GOYA* for the full on, no-holds-barred of the 'what' and the 'how' to do it.

So take heed of the advice given in the initial *GOYA*: turn off the *Today Programme* on Radio 4 and reduce your intake of the naysaying news media in general. We as normal people have the opportunity and freedom to try and shape our own lives and destinies now perhaps more than ever before. Before you start this book, take a few moments to quieten your mind and reflect on what is important for you and why... and then begin. This is the start of something special...

Tim Johnson
Director of Strategy
4Networking Ltd
www.StartAllOverAgain.co.uk

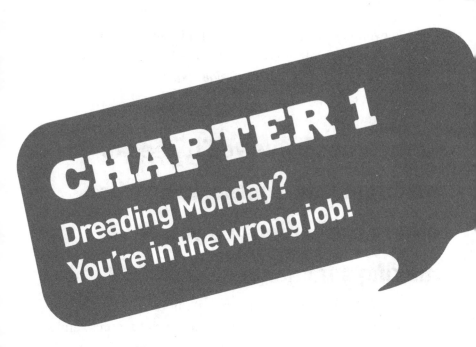

CHAPTER 1
Dreading Monday?
You're in the wrong job!

'm back.

You just don't know when you start something, whether it's going to work or not. My first book, *Get Off Your Arse (GOYA)* proved there's real value in being honest, being true.

It was a book that was penned with that in mind. It was written for those that would 'get it', not for those that wouldn't. Some hated it; most loved it.

At the time of publication of this book, *GOYA* has sold nearly 10,000 copies – which is just amazing for a first book. Apparently the average sales for a first book are somewhere around 300 copies.

We considered getting a publisher, but in keeping with the *GOYA* principles I thought, "We don't need a publisher; after all they would try imposing their values on us". The predictable "We'll need this taking out" and "You can't print that section" and so on.

We even had people in the book trade saying the title was too offensive for a biz book. If we'd listened to the "experts" you'd be reading *Get Off Your Backside Too*.

Snappy, eh?

So I ignored them.

Sometimes in life you'll need to maintain your course, even when others are telling you you're making a mistake.

I mean, how difficult can it be to 'publish' a book, when publishing is just writing, editing, design, printing, marketing and distribution? I've done all those things in my past.

So we kicked off our own publishing company, 4Publishing, and did just that.

I'll be honest – it proved to be a damn sight easier with a national business network of experts right at our fingertips.

OK, let's get going.

Honest is what I'd like you to be right now.

What's good in your life?

What's bad in your life?

How happy are you with your lot? Your life? Your relationships? Your job? Your business?

Think again. I want you to be really honest.

That's what *GOYA2* is about. Looking at life, relationships, business, sales and motivation… without the polish on.

There are new takes on some of the old themes, but we'll be looking at them from different perspectives. Fundamentally, the business lessons within this book work in day-to-day life and day-to-day life lessons cross over into business.

Over the course of the next fourteen chapters we're going to work together to bin the shitty stuff in your life, as it serves no purpose, and aim to replace it with good stuff that does work for you.

Net result? A happier, more successful you.

Less shit, more hit.

I've found my feet since writing my first book. Now I'm even more confident, bolder than before, so expect pretty radical stuff. You can also expect some explosive revelations about my life, which will help you with yours! For instance, I'll reveal the circumstances that resulted in gunshots being fired through the windows of my Manchester home.

More about the darkest days of my life in the next chapter...

So we're gonna revisit some old friends along with some new ones. I'll be talking with people who have experienced adversity, people who have used their fear as fuel, not as an excuse to roll over or hide, but to change direction, and who, like me, have used fear as the catalyst for a new beginning.

Denise McCallum, *www.detectivedenise.co.uk*, said

❝ I sat in one of your seminars where you said 'If you don't look forward to Monday mornings you're in the wrong job', so I went home and changed my job; in fact it might have taken me 18 months but now I've changed my whole life, thank you. ❞

We'll be also hearing from others who, as a result of reading *GOYA*, have moved their lives and businesses on, including winning new business by using some of my wacky business tips that are specifically designed to win attention. You'll just love the tip that gave an accountant who read something on my blog, FOUR – yes, that's one, two, three, four – new paying clients in a single month.

The tip will also work for you. So read on.

Powerful powerful stuff.

So strap yourself in right now and rather than our last time out, where we danced around the handbag for the first few chapters, this time out, straightaway I'll invite you back to mine for coffee.

So are you coming?

I met up with an old friend recently who told me how he was talking about dreading going to work on the Monday and was planning on throwing a 'sickie'. The weekend is notorious for hatching the first symptoms of what I call 'Monday flu'.

My friend has spent years in sales for his current company and as per the usual employee road map, has recently found himself increasingly pissed off with his role. So he did what any person would do in the same boat – spent his evenings trawling the jobs papers and his 'work days' trawling the job sites searching for the perfect job. He searched for months and months, and after months and months… no interviews.

Nope! No perfect role jumping off the job pages and tapping him on the shoulder, just frustration biting him on the arse.

So if you, like my friend, find yourself sitting there most days F5ing about, that is, pressing the F5 'refresh' key hoping for new leads, a new job or for something to come along to get you off your arse, then I've got news for you: nothing is going to happen. Nothing is going to change.

It's all down to you.

You need to change the somethings that you don't like about your current situation into somethings you do! And the archetypal dream of the "big country house and loads of money in the bank" success that currently eludes you may not actually be the success you might think.

Success is doing something you truly love and enjoy, and getting paid for it.

That's the secret of real success.

Belinda McCarthy, *www.belindamccarthy.co.uk*, shared her experiences with me...

66 I was an accountant – a pretty high ranking one at that, running a £50 million p.a. turnover business and holding the role of Financial Director.

Every day I'd go into the office, do my job, be proud of what I achieved. I did a damn good job. But I was constantly afraid that someone would suddenly point at me and say, 'You? You don't fit in here. You're just pretending.' I was afraid of being 'found out' for holding a post which actually didn't fit me, my personality and my aspirations at all.

I'd go home and cry, out of frustration, feeling that I was trapped in a role that paid me too much to leave, dreading a lifetime of Mondays doing a job which I was good at but felt no affinity with. Yet, one day, the scales metaphorically fell from my eyes. I realised that I could walk away any time I liked. I'd trapped myself, rather than the role trapping me. And once that mind-shift had happened, the world went from being scary on the 'outside' to the most exciting place possible. The lack of security, the new start – these were now not reasons to stay, but reasons to go. 99

There is nothing worse than working for years only to realise that your ladder to success is leaning against the wrong wall.

See, my work/life is so much fun because I've created that

work/life. No one was ever going to give me that 'perfect job': the one that involved swanning around the UK speaking at seminars and networking week after week, lunching with amazing people, falling over drunk on expenses with equally amazing people...

You know what, I'm a modern day Fonzie. You know that? But even so, I've still only got the second best job in the world. *Happy Days* indeed!

At the time of writing there wasn't a job title where you got paid for dicking about on Facebook, pretending to work. Well, not until 'Social Media Experts' invented themselves.

Are you a pirate?

Have you ever worn an eye patch?

Shouted "Pieces of eight?"

Does a parrot sit on your shoulder?

FACEBOOK PIRATE TEST RESULT

Congratulations! You're 63% a pirate! Woohoo – £13 quid!

Do you know that people get paid for Facebooking? I think their job title is 'disillusioned staffer'.

Going back to my current fun work/life, it has taken 5 years to create. That is, a life without the pressure of worrying about finances.

It wasn't always like that; I can vividly remember the days when nothing good came in the post. As in nothing, apart from official-looking letters with dark red mast heads and BIG CAPITAL LETTERS which told me I had seven days to pay £balance.

If that's where you are right now, paying the minimum payments to these guys, you may want to read the next bit with interest.

We need to have a two-pronged attack. We need to get your outgoing finances under control and your income increased.

Relieving financial pressure allows you to work smarter

and gain better clarity and focus.

I recall the fear when the 01244 (Chester-based 'debt collection' call centre, I'd later learn) number would appear on caller ID, leaving a firm and threatening voicemail message about my debt.

I'd call them up to explain I was struggling to pay. "Mr Burton, there is nothing we can do. Pay up or you'll go to court and you'll lose everything."

So the pressure built and, like so many people who have spent beyond their means, debt sneaked up on me... until I reached the moment when I recognised that the game was up.

Payday – SKINT – Payday – SKINT – Payday – SKINT

Stef Thomas, *www.noredbraces.co.uk*, says,

❝ Being employed is like being self-employed; the difference is you have one client. If suddenly that client decides they no longer need your services you're in trouble. ❞

My wife used to say that it's best being employed: "You know where you stand".

Erm! No you don't. If your boss decides he or she doesn't like you any more, it's over.

Going back to my mate...in his head the ideal solution for him was that he got made redundant and got a payoff. The employer's best outcome was that they got him on a dismissal or that he pissed off to another job so they wouldn't have to pay out redundancy.

As rot sets in on both sides, the game of 'Human Resource Cat n' Employee Mouse' begins...

"If you are that great a sales person, why not start your own business?" I suggested to him.

He told me that the company had blah blah blah and it was nothing to do with him. "Mismanagement means that loads of people are likely to be up for redundancy", he'd "see what happens when [if] that happens" and "I'll then see how much I get before making that call".

So you're telling me that you're a sales person responsible for massive sales? CORRECT.

So I hit him again, "Well, why not do it yourself if you're that good? Set up your own business and sell X".

"Erm well, I…" {insert waffle here}

Yeah. Yeah. Yeah.

Look, if you're really not cut out for self-employment, don't kid yourself, admit it now…

Employment's OK, but it's not for me any more since, like most that have experienced self-employment, I'm most likely unemployable. So, if staffing is a path you choose, it's best you do it properly and accept that someone is paying your wages plus NI plus pension plus expenses etc so that you do your job and do it well.

On the other side of the fence, as an employer, you'll often find your staff whingeing about you not paying and doing enough – they often don't realise that you have wider challenges.

Equally, it's not easy being an employee, but that is your choice, as is starting a business off.

You see, twice I was offered the opportunity to start my own business. Twice!

Both times I turned it down: stuff like VAT, accounts, P&L and end of year scared me to death. I just didn't understand it. The truth is, I still don't really… but I've got people around me that I trust and that do know about things financial.

When I tell people that, I see jaws drop and I think "old school thinking". The modern day MD doesn't need to have a three-piece suit, a pocket watch and an MBA. The modern MD has a team he trusts implicitly. Tamsen Garrie (Network Director of 4Networking) says that an old school boss says "Go", but a modern leader says "Let's go".

My role ain't bean counting – it's to lead from the front. The lesson is to focus on what you do best and surround yourself with people whose "what they do best" matches your blind and bored-shitless spots. That way you end up with a team with a graphic equaliser of strengths that you can tune to achieve things you couldn't do by yourself. That's where 4Networking (the networking organisation I head up) pays dividends – tens of thousands of people with different strengths right at your fingertips, so you can find and select your dream team for pretty much any weird and wonderful business ideas you may have.

In my experience, in the first few years of a new business you're playing at doing business anyways.

So get a bit radical, shake things up while you can still blame business naivety for any bad calls!

So – think about those things that are scaring you right now. Is it "losing my job" or "starting a business"? Dissect specifically which elements are concerning you. Then face those elements now.

Staring you right in the face is an opportunity. Every single piece of adversity in your life presents you with the option to change paths, to move in a different direction, and sometimes to start over again.

It was the fear of the unknown that had me defeated every time on the idea of starting a new business, with the result that I didn't get off my arse until the third time of kicking.

Is it that you need convincing to start your own business? After all, I too needed convincing. It's true... listen to this:

I dedicated *GOYA* to a man called Roy Hurley (erm, that's *GOYA#1* not *GOYA Too*... even I'm confused now)

Anyway, I met Roy Hurley on a computer game internet forum back in 2002. Roy lives in Australia and runs a successful engineering firm. We'd never met in real life, but talked often on the phone and MSN Messenger, and it was Roy that talked me into starting my own business.

Roy is the guy who changed my mind-set. He's the man that famously taught me that relationships are like bank accounts: withdrawals are OK, but stay in the black. I carry with me the bank account life lesson each and every day.

This is a man who gave so much when I had nothing to offer. All he asked was that I pay it forward and make a difference.

See, back in those days I was not in tiptop condition. I spent half my life worrying about paying debts and the other half worrying about not paying them. The credit card companies don't want to help you. While you're still paying, it's your problem; it's only at the point you stop paying them that the problem becomes theirs. It took me years to suss this out: that once I stopped paying they couldn't do anything!

As in nothing.

Yup! My credit rating was going to be goosed... but so what? I didn't really want any more credit, having got into a mess first time out.

Here's how I played it.

I recognised I could never ever sensibly clear down the debt since the interest alone was about 70% of my income.

So I stopped paying the minimum payments and went for a new minimum payment of £0.

At which point they contacted me. Remember earlier, they didn't want to negotiate?

I told them, "The pressure is making me ill and I've had to go to the doctor's".

I also went to the Citizens Advice Bureau, who suggested I tell my creditors to freeze my interest. Which they did, on all my debts!

Then, instead of being passively aggressive on the phone, the credit card boys started turning on the charm, issuing me with an income and expenditure form, which I completed. I had one credit card debt of £7,000 on which I had been paying something like £300 minimum payments each month with silly interest. This now went down to £27 a month with zero interest.

The debt was scheduled to be cleared in 2037.

But it gets better! After a while I received a letter offering me 50% off the debt if I made a full and final settlement. I ignored that letter and then a month or two later was offered 75% off if I settled in one lump.

Which I did.

Now look, the above not only reflects my personal experience but also that of others from within 4Networking whom I have encountered. It doesn't work so well with council tax or mortgage payments or secured debt. However, all these organisations will do something if contacted. The key requirement for these 'money off' plans is communication.

I have had years of worry about debt. So please learn from my experiences so that you don't have to. There is a way through any mountain of debt and at some point you need to scale that mountain, or do what I did and chop 75% off its height.

I am not encouraging irresponsible spending or pi

taking. No, I'm not. However, I am suggesting that if your debt has spiralled out of control with apparently no sensible way through it, then my experience may be a way forward.

There is no "life without risk".

I took a risk back in late 2004 when I walked out of a job to start my own business. I was 'coached' by Roy; he said, "The only one who doesn't believe in you... is you".

He talked me into taking that leap and if it were not for his words, you wouldn't be reading this book. The thing that changed in me was belief, as previously I had none. I had nil self-belief.

Conversely, with belief you are unstoppable. You can do anything. Well, you think you can... so go for it!

Right, now, we need to seek out those areas where you have little or nil self-belief. How powerful would you be if you had 100% belief in everything you did?

We're gonna work on that. I'll hold my hands up. I'm no expert in NLP, hypnotherapy, psychology and all that malarkey. I just draw on my experiences, and based on that I now recognise the immense power of believing in yourself.

Think of your business and life like a corkscrew: it's either "Going up or down... fast or slow..." /cue Barry White music.

The corkscrew is a really good metaphor to use when working out where you are in your life. Honestly, right now, my own corkscrew has never ascended so fast. A far cry from 5 years ago when I was going nowhere fast.

Something changed. I got off my arse. I stopped looking for excuses. I want you do the same.

I looked at what I could do right now and talked myself *into doing things* instead of talking myself *out of doing things*.

I was having some chill-out time recently playing my PlayStation 3 – that's my thing – and in the game I was playing I stumbled across a level which had five BIG super-mutant monsters in it. BAD muthas! So I retreated and began running away, with the intent of going to another level in order to find more powerful weaponry. The plan being to return later and take them on when I had the perfect 'loadout'.

My boy Ben (aged 6), watching me play, said, "Dad, why are you running? You have to believe in yourself." I thought, that's just nuts, I don't know where he got that from.

"OK son, I'll believe in myself and go for it..." Honestly, having played this game several times before, taking on five enemies at once was just suicide. I didn't have a chance. My prediction? A horrific and rapid demise but, hey, I'd humour my lad.

Supported and coached by my son, I ducked, dodged and fired back. Five minutes of intense combat later, the net result: the gang of super-mutants dead, with me bloodied, shot up and on my last legs and ammo.

But I'd defied my own logic and defied common sense, based on the words of a six year-old suggesting I "believe in myself". I'd done what I, the "experienced adult", had previously thought unthinkable, and won through.

I'd won through the situation without the perfect weaponry but with the support and what I thought to be the naive belief of someone.

This book is not some made-up kids' story. Some of it may sound unbelievable, but everything you will read in this book is true.

So – believe in yourself.

Set outrageous goals – ideally ones that make those around you think "You're mad!", and go for it.

I refer to these goals as 'batons of hope' because they carry you through to the next stage of your business and life.

I just asked my six year-old, "Who is the real voice of UK business?"

He said, "You, Dad."

Who am I to argue? After all, he was right last time.

Stop doubting and start believing in yourself. There is no downside.

Don't waste your life. Live it!

We're on the same team. I won't let you fail.

I have a *GOYA* attitude: I won't let myself fail.

Read those two lines through a few times. It'll prime you for what's to follow.

Go on, read it...

I'll wait.

Oh... you want to know what the best job in the world is?

A lap dance tester/Gregg's pasty tester (delete as applicable...)

CHAPTER 2 !

On New Year's Day 1995, I was a 21 year-old happy-go-lucky boy. By 2nd Jan I was shoved into a man's world.

This is undoubtedly the most hardcore chapter I've written so far in the *GOYA* series. It's about the part of my life that, up until now, I have kept to myself.

It's quite dark, but please plough on with it, as you'll see that good comes from bad situations (and normal mirth and jollity will return shortly).

I've always been the uncle who let my nieces stay up that extra half hour or snuck them a couple of *Jammy Dodgers* at bedtime. I'd always said if they ever got into any trouble or if there was anything they couldn't tell their mum or dad, they could always tell Uncle Brad and I'd sort it.

On the evening of Jan 1st 1995, I was smoking weed (that

was my thing back then) when I heard a knock at the door. Quickly getting rid of the joint, I went to answer the door. It was my eight year-old niece (let's call her 'Sandy') and she asked to have a word with me. I said, "Sure". Even through the haze of the marijuana I knew something serious was up.

She started the sentence, "Brad, you know when Geoff [name changed to protect the guilty] took me to his house? He-showed-me-the-bike-he's-bought-me-for-my-birthday-and-he-took-my-clothes-off-and-took-some-photos-but-you-can't-say-anything-because-he'll-beat-you-up-he-showed-me-a-knuckleduster-and-told-me-I-mustn't-say-anything-to-anyone-otherwise-you-will-end-up-in-hospital."

My blood turned icy. Bastard! Geoff was a former pro boxer and a close friend of the family. A very dangerous one. Someone who had a rap sheet as long as his arm: possession of firearms, armed robbery and so on. That was the norm in that part of Manchester. Knowing people like him was almost a badge of honour.

This was a man who in the past had dated my sister and guided me as a father figure after my real dad left when I was six months old.

I had 3 options as I saw it:

1) Go after him myself – likely to be most people's reaction. "I'll KILL him."

2) Ask Sandy to say nothing. We'd both carry the secret for years.

3) Go to the police.

The only sensible option was to go to the police.

I said to Sandy, "Thanks for telling me. No, you won't have to see him again. We'll sort this. Thanks for telling me. Wait here…" My sister and mum were at a house party opposite. I went over and explained. The party atmosphere dropped away and the tears started.

That night, I began smoking 'normal' cigs.

Sandy had evidence of the offence – which she shared. The police needed to get Social Services involved. The police couldn't rouse them for a few days because of the holiday break.

We were advised to pretend to continue as normal. If we spoke with Geoff we were not to let on about anything at all until Social Services had interviewed Sandy.

Sandy, along with her older (aged 11) sister, went to stay with their dad for a week or so. Over the course of the next few days the family cried, drank, argued, hugged, fought, and there was the inevitable "How could we let this happen?" and so on.

Then, on the 6th January, the day before Sandy's birthday, my sister's doorbell rang.

I answered the door. It was Geoff. He'd called to drop round the bike he'd promised my niece for her 9th birthday. I took the bike and escorted him upstairs.

Sandy's mum opened the door and asked who was at the door. I replied, "Geoff. He's brought round Sandy's present".

That was the trigger. "GET THAT DIRTY BASTARD OUT OF MY HOUSE!!"

Geoff asked, "What was that about?"

I said, "She's been drinking. Best go. I'll ring you later". I never did make that call. In fact I never spoke to him again.

After the Social Services had returned to work, interviews were done, evidence and statements gathered, child protection officers assigned.

Geoff went on the run. He knew the game was up the minute he turned up at my sister's house and would communicate with the police for the next few weeks via his solicitor. Subsequently he handed himself in, was charged and went straight to prison on remand while he awaited trial.

During the same period of time I'd received all manner of death threats, really chilling ones, encouraging me to drop the case. One night I remember ringing my brother, crying. I thought it was the last time I would speak to him. I had been tipped off that I was going to be killed that night. I was terrified. Depression, fear, and the anticipation of death made me ill.

Remember, I was 21 years old. Can you recall your life at that age? I hope it was fun and carefree. Mine wasn't.

My family was living in fear… My sister stayed at mine with the kids, along with my mum. Each evening I'd place a bookcase behind the front door. I had a paint tray full of half gloss paint/half turps which I would rest midway up the stairs. I figured if someone got covered in that, even if they ran away they'd be much easier to detect.

Extreme situations require extreme solutions.

Then it went from really bad to much, much worse. Early one morning I was woken by a call. The police officer told me, "There has been a shooting at your house, but you're not to panic."

"Is everyone alright?" I asked.

"Yes. No one has been hit. Naturally they're shaken up, but no one has been hit."

I found out later that my nieces (who, remember, were eight and eleven years old) were awoken by gunshots and smashing glass. Screaming and shaking with fear, they crawled onto the landing.

It ended as fast as it began. However, the knock-on effects of those few seconds continue to be felt a full fifteen years on.

Arriving by taxi at the top of my Coronation Street-like street, I was greeted by police who had sealed off the street, helpfully armed with Heckler & Koch sub-machine guns.

Forensics had been through my bedroom and found two 9mm bullets.

That morning my family went into a police witness protection programme. Changing their names, they were moved into a tatty, flea-ridden (literally) 'safe house'.

I didn't join them. I went to live with my girlfriend (at the time). More about that later.

People often ask me if 'Brad Burton' is my real name... as it sounds like a stage name. Well it really is Brad Burton and has been since '73.

I'd gone from being a homeowner, pothead, computer games journalist, to being homeless, jobless and having a family unit which had to split up. I had become the 'head man' of my immediate family at just twenty one.

I filled a holdall with clothes, including a few sentimental items and that was it. A modern day *Mary Celeste* for any future buyer.

I left my two-bed terraced house exactly as it was. I left all the furniture and walked away from equity and mortgage – the lot. My place of birth and home town for twenty one years, Salford, was no longer "home". Through no fault of my own I had become a fugitive on the run.

Nothing mattered anymore, including everything that had been so important before the shooting – even my pride-and-joy *Sega Mega Drive* and thirty or so games.

Looking back now, this in a way prepared me for the rest of my life. The realisation that the only things that matter, as in really matter when we strip all the bullshit away, are love, family, friends, health and safety.

I had four of those five.

The gunman, needless to say, was never found, and since, at the time of the shooting, Geoff was being held at Her Majesty's Pleasure, no charges could be brought with regard to the shooting.

Geoff was, however, charged with offences relating to the incident involving my niece, and a court date was set. This was followed by adjournment after adjournment because the 'other side' created as many hurdles and upsets as possible, in the hope we'd drop the case.

Yeah, we thought of doing that, of course.

You will know from your own life that some things are worth fighting for and this was one of those.

On the final day of the case, the police picked us up in one of those vans with the blacked out windows. Nobody talked. It was like riding to a funeral in a limousine.

We drove in through an underground entrance and my family were held in a secure area at the rear of the courts. We were chaperoned by an undercover policewoman – a Child Protection Officer – who had been assigned to us since day one. Her name was 'Jackie M'. She was an absolute angel; the pressure of dealing with cases of this nature day in, day out must weigh heavy.

I asked her, "Can I go into the court room?" She said, "If you really want to. I'll come with you – just in case."

In case of what? It's a court!

So we walked to the front and I was now standing outside the courtroom where there must have been thirty or so people waiting to go into court for the next case.

Or so I thought.

Then it dawned on me that they weren't waiting to go into court – they were supporters of Geoff.

When people realised who I was it got very fiery very fast, with all manner of people up in my face. Geoff had told them that I'd trumped up the charges because I'd owed him money for drugs.

The truth no longer mattered. He who controlled the

violence controlled the flow of information. I often think that under different circumstances that could have been me outside court, supporting Geoff in the face of a 'Brad Burton' who had *stitched up* the former father figure in my life.

Geoff rushed out of the courtroom, banging open the door. My foot stopped the flying door hitting my face. The case had been thrown out on a legal technicality. Apparently my niece was "coached". Geoff's barrister told the judge that his client had been painted as a "big bad wolf". If my memory serves me correctly this was one of the first times a video link for evidence had been used, so the social workers had spent time with my niece, practising using the Little Red Riding Hood story on a dummy TV video link. So this was yet another kick in the teeth for the family that had lost so much and gained nothing from this whole situation.

Even though the outcome panned out the way it did, it had still been the right thing to do. The bravery and resolve of the entire family and in particular the then eight year-old Sandy puts things in perspective for me each and every time.

A friend of mine, Brendan Johnson, *www.outsidetheasylum.eu*, shared with me his thoughts:

❝ Getting told you might not have a tomorrow makes you realise that today is all you have. Be grateful for all the bad days, as well as the good – they make you what you are.

If you ARE having a bad time, know this. It WILL change... and if you think things can't get any worse, you probably don't understand the situation! ❞

To add to all that, my girlfriend at the time was pregnant – all wrong, too much too soon and besides which we were together for all the wrong reasons. However, I went to live with her about thirty miles out of the way.

It didn't work out.

We all have a story. Each of us has things in our life that hold us back.

We are often mentally anchored to past events or situations that have caused us pain or fear – things that prevent us from moving forward freely in the here and now.

Think about the anchor in your past that is holding you back... Is it really essential any more or is it stopping you moving your life on and finally closing that chapter in your book?

Something else I've never shared with anyone outside my close friends and family is that I've a son in Manchester that I'd not seen in thirteen years. Through no fault of his nor mine we'd lost contact.

It went something like this... If I didn't marry his mum, I'd never see my boy again. As you can appreciate this was not the ideal foundation for a future relationship.

Extreme circumstances had kicked in back then. I had now signed on the dole and I'd drive a five hundred mile round trip in a borrowed car for a 'supervised visit with a court welfare officer', to be told my son was "poorly". This happened three times. An obstructive and destructive 'ex' didn't make for the best of circumstances. I was, apparently, considered "a direct danger" to my son. His mother even used the shooting as the reason why I was a "bad father", inferring to the courts that I was involved in drug dealing, hence the shooting, and implying that gang warfare would be a continuing threat to my son's safety.

It was an out-and-out lie and hurt like hell, especially since I'd helped her deal with so many of her personal demons.

Whilst writing this, something has just dawned on me! A lot of people have told me things about their life which they haven't told anyone else and I've always looked to help where help was needed. I must have one of those "to be trusted" faces.

The last time I had seen my son was on his first birthday. He was tired and didn't know who the strange man trying to give him a "tickle me, Elmo" was.

I did everything within my power legally, going to court on numerous occasions to gain contact and parental responsibility orders. I was granted the orders and yet the courts seemed unwilling to enforce them.

I made the decision to pull back, because it wasn't helping anyone.

So when I see members of *Fathers 4 Justice* holding up traffic, freezing for hours on motorway bridges dressed as Spiderman, I admire them for continuing the struggle the only way left to them when the legal system fails forcibly estranged fathers and their children.

Since the day I had last seen my son in 1997, there had been a nagging hurt every day. Every Christmas Day since, I'd cry too. The tears were for my loss, but also for my son's (let's call him 'D'), who didn't have his Dad there with him on each of those Christmas Days to spoil him with toys, cuddles, selection boxes and just the normal growing up stuff.

I knew that in business, in life (and I guess, while driving) constantly looking in the rear view mirror doesn't help you to move forward with confidence and conviction.

So I stowed all those feelings away. Only those closest to me were aware of them.

When we started 4Networking back in 2006, I'd had enough of running and being pushed around by bullies. Hence the reason I said to myself, "You want to fight dirty? Let's do it."

I believe hand-on-heart that's why I'm so passionate about 4N. Here was my vehicle to finally make a stand, to go against all the odds, to turn and face the bullies and say, "I run from *nothing*. You want a fight? *Bring it on!*"

By now you should be able to see why I live life the way I do – with a smile. When you've stood on the edge of the abyss, where you genuinely believe you're on borrowed time, you find beauty and happiness in the simplest things.

For instance, I make calls about the 4N business the likes of which only someone who has visited the abyss would contemplate.

I could risk it all. I had nothing, I'd never amounted to anything, so I couldn't lose.

The old school, well-established rival organisation who called me out back then, found that they had picked the wrong person to fight at the wrong time. I'd had enough of running. This was now my time to fire back.

Your past can help steer your future.

No matter how painful things are, things which make no sense at the time, they will eventually make complete sense.

Ian Beardsall, K&R Consultancy *www.kandrcounselling. co.uk*, is a therapist who deals with all manner of trauma. Ian shared with me a wonderful analogy.

❝ Imagine you were a passenger on the *Titanic*. The ship hits the iceberg. One lifeboat is filled with 'SURVIVORS'. They

spend days replaying the horrible event in their mind over and over again, bobbing about on the water, making no progress.

Another lifeboat is filled with 'THRIVERS'. These guys briefly revisit the event which got them there but then they begin to paddle to shore. Hitting the iceberg wasn't their fault and there's nothing they could have done to avoid it. It was out of their control. However, they have taken control of their future. **"**

I just love that. Thanks, Ian.

A few weeks ago I had lunch with my friend Shaa Wasmund (*www.shaawasmund.com*). A woman who's a first class business woman with a massive work ethic. In fact massive ethics full stop. She's the PR genius behind the Dyson launch. A loony boxing fan, she also used to handle Chris Eubank's PR back in the day. Like Shaa, I'm also a loony boxing fan so we clicked – waffling about boxing for thirty five minutes the first time we met.

Over lunch we moved onto talking about motivation and how it's all about "seizing the moment". She shared with me the story about her partner, who had recently been tragically killed in a car crash. Inside one minute of Shaa's and her four year-old son's lives, everything changed. In the blink of an eye, their lives had been tipped into a different landscape.

I shared with Shaa my story of how I'd lost contact with my son 'D'. She said, "Can I ask you two questions?"

Question one. "God forbid that something should happen to 'D', but if it did, and you then never had the chance to say the things you wanted to say, how would you feel?"

Shit!

Question two. "If you were 'D', what would you want your dad to do?"

Find me...

She must have read my face. "There's your answer".

In that minute the decision was made. Thank you, Shaa – *http://twitter.com/shaawasmund*

So, I put out a tweet to my followers for a private investigator and 4Networker Denise McCallum steps forward, *http://twitter.com/InvestigateUK*

Within minutes Denise tracked down 'D''s mum. Both address and contact numbers, and found her on Facebook. Then during the big Facebook changeover earlier this year, which took a couple of weeks, 'D''s mum disappeared while Facebook sorted itself out.

I spent that time thinking about the approach I should take in order to make it happen. I thought – you know what? A Facebook message would allow me to make a clinical and unemotional approach.

Then two days later, I walked into the kitchen and my wife, who has wiped my tears and shared my anguish over the last thirteen years, asked "Brad, have you seen your Facebook?"

"No. Why?"

"'D' has added you as a friend."

"No way! Shut the fuck up!"

"Seriously! Look!" insisted Kerry.

And sure enough – that's how it happened.

Fourteen years in the making and 'D' finds and makes contact with me within two weeks of *me* finding *him*. Sounds a bit 'cosmic order'-y and 'Law of Attraction' (and, let's face it, you couldn't make it up! Maybe there is something in cosmic orders and the Law of Attraction).

This social media thing is more than "I've just walked the dog, lol".

It's re-connecting people, re-connecting friends and, most importantly for my situation, re-connecting families.

So, if you have something or someone in your life, and you've lost contact with them for whatever reason – make contact today: win, lose or draw, you will know!

'D''s dad was back in his life, as I had always intended to be.

Don't let people from your past worry you. There's a reason why they play no part in your future. However, some of the lessons from the past, no matter how painful, can shape your life positively, and in ways you wouldn't think possible.

So that's the heavy chapter nearly out the way. We can move onto some wonderful, lighter, fun stuff again! Recognise that whatever you've gone through, you are not alone. You are, however, one of the lucky ones. A 'Thriver' who can use the pain of your past to make a positive and lasting difference to those you love.

You know, even taking into account everything that's happened, I wouldn't change a single thing. Why? Because it brings us to where we are today –

if it wasn't for my darkest days, would you be reading this book, this chapter? Nope.

Who knows what my alternative life would have held, or indeed what you would be doing right now instead of reading this book!

Weird, isn't it? Anyways, I hope this part of my story is making you feel better about any adversity you've encountered or are currently going through.

You are not alone. You can win through.

RELAX

IT'LL PASS

CHAPTER 3
Sail up, anchor down

There was Graham, explaining to me why he couldn't get somewhere. "It's half an hour away in the car, and my car has no MOT", he complained.

"Buy a bike. You could do with losing some weight anyway, Slim," I said.

You may be wondering who Graham is. Let me explain. He posted on the *www.4networking.biz/forum*, the 4N online community, about how his business situation was getting tough.

I decided to put a call in. He was slipping. That's the term I use to describe when someone is running out of lies, including lying to themselves. Graham had started his own business a year or so ago. Things business-wise were not going well for him but he was either over-playing the optimism card or delusional – depends whether you want to view it tender or tough. He had even gone so far as to pretend to the wife that he had business appointments when in fact he was sitting in hotel lobbies all day "dicking about".

He had no idea what to do, apart from looking busy by wearing a suit and tie each day.

Meanwhile his wife was actually busy, working at a care home and being the primary breadwinner. He was also the carer for his deaf brother and in addition managed all his brother's finances.

You can see where this is going.

He confided that he'd "borrowed" £800 of his deaf brother's rent money. The money that Graham looked after. G was responsible for paying his brother's landlord. With his brother's rent now nearly three months in arrears, it wouldn't be long before his brother would face an eviction notice.

So not only was this man fibbing to his wife and brother, the pressure and the guilt was building up, resulting in a feeling of total helplessness.

Desperate people do desperate things – and generally the wrong things.

First thing I did on that first call was tell him that his own situation was a secondary consideration. Graham's first responsibility was to his brother. He needed to speak to his brother's landlord and come clean. He did just that. You know what? The landlord was cool about Graham's situation, admired his honesty, accepted a payment plan and didn't evict Graham's brother.

An action led to an outcome.

Looking at that, and similar situations, it is the anticipation and the fear that creases you. Remember the previous chapter? It's the difficult circumstances that leave you paralysed and create inertia and inaction.

I sent Graham a copy of *GOYA* and asked him to read it – which he did over the weekend. I then arranged to meet – which we did. He had fifteen minutes of hardcore, mental beating up from me. A 'deconstruction' which is often needed in order to begin a rebuild on clean ground.

I then checked in by phone every single week which followed... until finally he landed his dream job as a web designer. Guess what? He cycles to the train station every day and he loves it.

There is rarely a bad situation in biz without a solution.

Graham started to sort out his life by pulling up the anchor (the things holding him back) and by getting a sense of direction (putting up the sail). He needed something to provide wind to his sail to get him moving where he needed to go – in his case the wind was paid employment.

He calls me a "lifesaver" – and I have to admit I like that. Maybe it's bit strong, but you just don't know what people might do when they can't see a way out of their inaction for themselves. When things get on top of people, they sometimes think extreme thoughts.

I know I have in my past.

Anyway, a life which was slipping has changed direction as a result of taking action and is now sailing in the right direction.

It's never too late to change direction... never

Why would I help a guy who wasn't even a paid 4N member? Why? It was the right thing to do. That's why. So if you can make a huge impact on someone's life with little investment on your part – do it.

You can't help everyone. That may be difficult to accept, but you need to be realistic. You can, however, look after your tribe. How you define who is in your tribe is down to you. For me, it's those I can positively touch and who I look to for support, friendship, fun and advice. In other words, people who 'get' me.

"Lifesaver"… when your head's down, you may find yourself talking about wanting change and yet simultaneously avoiding it like hell.

It's only you holding yourself back, often as a result of having your anchor down. Why is that? What's being achieved by just holding your current ground? If you're anchored where you are while you formulate a plan, then that's OK, I'll let you off… for the time being.

Rooted to the spot with no idea of direction is not OK.

With your sail up, what do you want to achieve? OK. Plan your passage, lift anchor and head for your destination.

So, stop reading for a sec.

What is your destination? Think about it.

Mike Bailey, *www.facebook.com/promotebusiness* said,

66 Some people will remain in port, tied up and safe, until the perfect day dawns, calm flat as a pancake sea, azure blue sky, not a breath of wind. Then and only then will they dare to set sail, off they go out of the harbour…ahh, but they can't can they, there's no wind, they can't move, they've got that perfect day that they've been waiting for and realised only then, too late, that it's not perfection. It never is and it never will be.

Just what have they been missing out on all that time? They were waiting for something that will never come. 99

Once you've sussed out where you want to go, you are likely to encounter all sorts of people who can accelerate your journey. Some may even get you there pretty much instantly, provided you pay them enough!

OK, paying your way into instant paradise is generally cobblers. You may want to believe that some fast-track route to success exists, using a *Success Sherpa* or marketing guru who claims to be able to accelerate you to where you want to be, all travelling together on a magic carpet of PR to overnight success.

The reality is that your destination is going to take some time to reach. Sailing boats are more realistically affordable than rockets for most people. And yet I see people who are duped into buying things which will supposedly magically take them to their business and personal heaven in an instant.

Advertising, PR, email marketing and telemarketing are all great provided you can afford for them NOT to work.

I've just come off the phone to someone who asked my advice on £2,000 of advertising they had been offered.

I told them they'd be better off printing their web address on two hundred tenners and chucking them down Oxford Street on a busy Saturday morning, recording, YouTubing and 'viraling' the chaos that would unfold. Spending money is too easy – make sure you really know what you are getting for your money.

No matter what anyone tells you, right now there is no business Star Trek *Teleporter* which takes you to a world of instant riches.

Which gets me thinking – I've yet to meet anyone who is rich as a result of a *Get Rich Quick* scheme. I have, though, met many who've been stripped to their uppers or at best left out of pocket as a result of *Get Rich Quick* schemes. *Get Un-rich Quick* scheme or *Get Some Other Thieving, Manipulative Bastard Rich* scheme is more like it.

Get Un-rich Quick schemes can be identified easily by visiting a web page where you need a trusty mouse wheel to scroll down and down and down and down the page, interspersed with regular claims like this – *"Learn the secrets that will increase your sales by 2,567% – in just 2 days!"*

After about ten minutes of mouse-wheeling, you're rewarded with the opportunity of watching a "short" twenty-five minute video.

If you are daft (and gullible) enough to keep scrolling for ten minutes and then watch the "short" video, they've got you anyways. *It's all a LOAD OF BOLLOCKS!!!*

Since we began 4Networking it has become the fastest growing business breakfast network in the world – and there has not been one single thing in the history of the company and *Brand Brad* that has worked. Fortunately, the anticipated big leap wasn't business critical. But imagine if it was... if we'd spent £10k on a media campaign, that just had to work!

What can happen in business is that you plough energy, resources and, just as painfully, your hopes, into advertising, direct mail campaigns and so on, and then end up deflated when they don't give you the results you expect or have been *sold* to expect.

So, don't rely on one thing or one person for your success, whether that's marketing activity or a mentor, because in general you'll end up disappointed. Those activities, which cost you in both resources and hope, can set you back financially and mentally, rather than set you up.

Rely on self... it's down to you.

Once again, it's the old adage, "little and often", that brought both me and 4Networking to where we are today. It's the result of lots of mistakes, lots of decisions, lots of changes lots of times.

I recently spoke with someone who is paying a *Millionaire Maker* £16,000 per year for a mentoring programme. What a load of shit! The only one who is "making a million" is the mentor. Honestly, there are no fast-track, easy routes to success and wealth. None.

Factors like economic conditions, saleable products and shed-loads of luck are vital. When I come across these so-called *Millionaire Maker* mentors, I always make it my business to find out how they made their money. When you dig you find not a single one of them did it overnight.

The way they did it is exactly the same as us with 4Networking: lots of decisions and lots of mistakes, many times over. So, before you go running to the front of a *Millionaire Maker* auditorium waving your cheque book, ask yourself, do you really want a millionaire mind-set?

What exactly are you buying?

Money isn't everything, although not having it is. I would coach you to find something positive out of any negative. At the time it may not seem like it, but there is real value to be gained from hurdles, setbacks, disappointments and other challenges in your life.

That's the real key to millionairedom. Finding the positives in the negatives from adapting unworkable ideas into workable ones.

You can probably do it all yourself. That's if money to

millionairedom is what you really want. The difference is, rather than paying someone £16,000 a year, you need to do it for yourself.

The extract below is taken from a conversation I had with someone who signed up for one of these seriously expensive *Success Programmes*:

~~~~~~

❝ I signed up, but regretted it and cancelled within a month. I just got fed up with the "him, him, him" aspect. He sells places at his summit and takes thirty minutes to tell you that he will tell you "something worthwhile". You then hang on and on waiting to hear this 'nugget', only to get really fed up when he spends another yet thirty minutes talking around the subject. He then finishes off by telling you that you will "find out" if you attend his Summit!!

Some of his stuff is great and there are a few gems buried in it, but I just kept wanting to shout, "Get to the bloody point"! I reckon if you're the kind of person who's got the get-up-and-go to rustle up a considerable amount of cash and pitch up at his 'Summit', you're probably going to do well in business anyway. ❞

~~~~~~

The same goes for franchised business coaches. A three-week course and an online resource doesn't INSTANTLY make you a great business coach.

You need some real world experience complete with scars and that can't just be taught.

Tipping up in an F-reg *Astra* and trying to talk your way into £1,500 a month retainer is not clever. By the way, that's a real example that I've seen with my own eyes.

Broad brush: 'Old School' consultancy is struggling. Back in good old 2005 it was all about paying for information. Now that same information is available free online. The world is changing.

One company I know was turned down for a bank loan by a sharp bank manager who noted that if they could afford to spend £1,500 a month on a consultant, they were not yet in need of a bank loan. The point is, if you can genuinely afford £1,500 a month, you probably don't need a consultant.

Ultimately, success is down to you.

That's it. Hard work, a lot of it, the ability to get back on your feet having just been knocked on your arse... again! A focus on your destination, with plenty of sacrifices to get there, and a smattering of luck.

In *GOYA* I mentioned that being in business isn't just about private number plates, fish tanks and spinny chairs. Those are the fun trappings of business, but just because you have them doesn't mean you have a business. Since mentioning that tick list in *GOYA*, I'll admit that personally, all I need now is a fish tank in the office to complete the set. I don't let that stuff distract me though...

If I said to you, "Here's a direct sales job which involves door knocking, but after a slow first year you should earn £25,000 a year. Oh, by the way, you have to do eighty-hour weeks for ever more". What would you say?

"On your bike", probably.

However, when exactly the same rubbish deal is wrapped up as a "franchise opportunity", people willingly pay £30,000 for it.

Someone asked me, "Is 4N MLM friendly?" Answer: "Absolutely". So long as you have a great product, 4N is a fab place for Multi Level Marketing (MLM) and for MLMers to sell their stuff and their *Get Rich Quick* schemes.

Some people are never happier than when they've just missed the bus. In a perverse way some even get involved in self-sabotage. I'm not in a position to criticise – I've done it too. Yup, that's true. I hung onto those daft working class values much longer than I should have –

five years on I'm still waiting for someone to "find me out".

The old ways are dead. Businesses which are living in the past, sticking to the old ways of doing things, are being left behind. The massive growth of 4N has been down to us looking at the whole biz networking thing in a new way, with different eyes.

If you stick with the same old dead horse, try as you might by, let's say by getting a different jockey or a bigger whip, you're still flogging a dead horse.

It's that reason that probably allowed me to say, "You know what? Being skint, having no money, ain't nowhere near as bad as having been shot at". So my ability to deal with the stuff I needed to deal with when running a business, as in 3 days 'til mortgage payments kinda isn't the big deal fear-wise that it would be for most people.

I only started getting serious about life after I reached thirty or so, at about the same time my current crop of kids came along. All of a sudden natural sand barriers have to be formed as life moves along.

The problem with "anchor down, sail up" is that you have a bad time being blown about by circumstances, but end up not going anywhere. You need to take control of your direction, rather than meander aimlessly from one opportunity to another. Make your own future, rather than as I did at first, waiting for someone else to gift it me.

It's never too late to change direction… never

You will find the strength needed. Holding onto something can make you feel safe, and give you strength. I have an eagle made in the late '70s out of plaster and sprayed gold. For me, it's a relic that makes me feel safe. I can look towards it and find strength. Sounds a bit wacky, but you will also have a place, person or thing that you visit or talk to which gives you enough 'certainty' to feel safe and to make that decision needed to move on.

I worked recently with someone on a three month £4,000 'programme'. Afterwards, I grabbed my calculator and worked out the pay at £175 per hour.

Was it worth it? Possibly. It was certainly more palatable and easy to swallow by being wrapped up as a three month 'programme'. All of a sudden it became good value.

Same prezzie, different wrapping paper.

Sometimes you don't need gurus charging you loads of money on 'mentoring programmes'; you need energy, pace, self-belief and people around you who you can trust. People who have no agenda other than to see you succeed and flourish.

Anyone that knows me, knows that deep down, that's what I want. To help make a difference.

So, back to getting your anchor raised. You need to suss first where you are going. And then suss out what's anchoring you down.

You have one life. Don't waste it travelling somewhere you don't want to go.

I'm typing this sitting in the garden. It's wonderfully peaceful on a summer's evening, the sun's going down, the chill's just picking up. I can hear the tweets of the birds, interspersed with raised voices: "KILL THE BLUE GUY. I'M GOING TO TRY TO GET THE ARMOUR. COVER ME."

No, I'm not going doolally. The sounds are from the open window of D's bedroom. The son who I'd not seen for thirteen years up until this year. He now lives with his dad, and he's XBoxing.

When I think back about my life as I'm typing this, it all makes sense. The madness of the past brings together converging paths. Things are working out right now, and the future? Who knows? But it's "all about now" – you need to enjoy the journey as much as the destination.

Earlier today I visited my granddad, now 87, born in 1922.

I told him that 2010 had been the best year of my life so far. I asked him if he could remember what his best year had been. He fired back instantly, "I haven't had it yet!"

Just awesome. I hope that comment generates as big a smile in your mind as I enjoyed in mine.

You have to trust that things will just sort themselves out. You can't speed up progress in your life, in the same way you can't go on a *Millionaire Mentoring Programme* and become a millionaire. But you can change direction and accept that every single step you take from that moment on is towards that new life where you want to be.

You have to make decisions. Good ones and bad ones.

And you have to learn from every one of them.

I didn't know where I wanted to be. All I knew was that after everything I'd been through I deserved some success. I never thought I'd have a home like I do. It's not, as I put out on twitter, "A castle with a drawbridge". It's a five-bedroom house in Somerset.

I'll say it again, I wouldn't change a single thing...

Same goes for Tim.

You know Tim Johnson's story, don't you? He's the Director of Strategy for 4N and he's got one arm.

Tim Johnson had it all... big house, big car, directorship of a big business and an equally big, bad attitude.

He took a BIG corner in his BIG car too fast, had a BIG crash, lost his arm, contracted the MRSA bug, nearly died. Pushed out of his business, got addicted to painkillers (morphine), went to uni, took an MBA, put numerous further failed businesses behind him. All inside eight years.

His arm and his high-rolling business gone, and nearly for a while his marriage, but he says it's a fair swap for the life he now leads. He's doing what he loves, devising the forward looking strategy for a forward looking organisation! That would never have happened had he not gone through all of the above.

My mum says no matter how bad things get, they could always be worse. Don't believe her. Try sitting yourself on a bacon slicer...

Let's look at my life in a nutshell. Bullets, move to Somerset, meet wifey, start a great family, start my own biz. D's back in my life and living with me. Fifteen years in the making.

The thing about the past is that you can let it screw up your future...but only if you let it.

We all lose our way in life, only to find it again.

By now you've sussed out where we're heading... I say "we're" because I'm coming along for the ride. It's an exciting future you have ahead.

I'll lift the anchor, you raise the sail.

It's time to set sail.

CHAPTER 4
Does gym membership make you fit?

My fitness sucked. Frankly, I was more a running-a-bath sort of guy rather than running around a football field, but there comes a point where you have to take action. They say that life begins at 40. In my case it was 40" elasticated waist Millets jeans. Not a great look to be rocking at 37.

So I got me a personal trainer, Justin Dodd, *www. evolvetraininguk.co.uk*. I said "running" earlier. At one point "running", in my case, was literally being pushed around a field.

Horrid. Horrid. Horrid.

Then suddenly six months has passed and I no longer find it horrid. I wouldn't go as far as to say I enjoy it. But it works. I quite like being alive. Eating four full English breakfasts each week at 4Networking events for about four years takes its toll on your body. It's no accident that I'm this fat. *Boom boom*.

In my game breakfast scoffing is an "occupational hazard."

The upside of any 4N member's expanding waistline is an expanding contact and business base.

One day, during a board meeting, it was mentioned that for some members, 4Networking "isn't working" and this got us scratching our heads. Wtf?

Then Tim Johnson said that some people think it's a vending machine: you put your money in and out comes a load of work. Life and 4N are not like that. "It's more like a gym for businesses", said Tamsen Garrie, 4N Network Director.

Terry Cooper, our Development Director, just nodded as he does... sagely.

"It's more like a gym for businesses." I do like that.

Prior to being shoved around fields, I had a real gym membership. About £40 per month paid by direct debit. The problem was, like most people, I rarely went. On the odd occasion when I did, I spent time, using the floor-to-ceiling mirrors, stealing glances at the women's aerobics classes.

Stop the press. I'm a bloke.

Or listening to my mp3 player... or yakking to the gym rats about the latest food supplements and training techniques.

Very little time was actually spent on the equipment, pushing weights or hitting the punch bags. Don't even talk to me about the rowing machines.

Twenty minutes of cardiovascular exercise and you've managed to burn off the calories of half a pink wafer biscuit.

Totally demoralising.

So, surprise surprise, over the six months of gym membership, I'd made little or no progress and therefore did what so many do – I cancelled the direct debit.

Was that the gym's fault or mine?

Dave Bradburn, *www.opuscreative.co.uk* has this to say:

" Gym membership can be a bit of a red herring – it can even have a negative effect and lead to complacency if someone thinks that by paying up they've ticked that box. Only when linked to motivation, the correct attitude and a substantial amount of effort will it give you fitness. The hardest part of that whole process often comes after you've paid for the membership – when you've got a hundred and one other things to do, it's a miserable day and you feel like you're going to look like an idiot walking out of the changing rooms and into the gym. Get through that and make it part of your normal routine and it will start to work for you. "

If we accept that networking organisation memberships are, in many respects, equivalent to that of a gym, in order for you really to get the best from networking, for a kick-off you need to attend. When you attend, you have the chance to work it. That doesn't mean going into full-on selling mode because, as you may have found out, that really doesn't work.

Working it means using your time not only to learn about other members' companies and products, but also to discover your own personal and business strengths and weaknesses. Doing this will help to increase your chances of 'pumping up' your business success. Even I'm getting bored with the gym metaphor now...

Let's try another one.

Networking is a bit like making jelly.

Stick with this: it will make complete sense... probably.

Back to the jelly, we made one over the weekend. Yup, that's right. Helping my 6 year-old boy, I got some strawberry jelly cubes, poured boiling water into an upside down rabbit mould, whacked it into the fridge and waited for it to set...

Well, at least I did. My lad had a different strategy. Namely, opening the fridge door every five minutes, poking his finger in and asking, "Is it ready yet?"

Each time he came away disappointed, because his jelly hadn't set.

I explained that no amount of wishing it to set would speed the process up. In fact, constant opening of the fridge door was slowing down the setting process.

Are you doing that with your networking? Slowing down the process of your relationship building by constantly questioning whether it's working or not? Networking is not about sales and it's not about products. It's about people and relationships with those people.

Get the people bit right, the sales follow.

There is so much more to it than out-and-out sales, so, if prior to reading this chapter you found yourself sitting at a desk at the end of each week armed with squared paper, a scientific calculator and a pencil in your mouth fanatically trying to work out your ROI on networking, then sorry, but networking clearly isn't for you.

Well, it probably is, but you just need to change your approach. Otherwise, you are going to end up disappointed and be 'deselected' by a load of people in the process.

If you get networking right, life and business gets so much

easier. You create a tribe of advocates, a virtual company of suppliers, gain clients and some of those become fans.

✱ Those people that leave after 6 months, saying "It's not worked" or "I got nothing from it" have totally missed the point.

If they did attend regularly, they will have achieved something from it or been blind and chosen to ignore the benefits.

I spoke with sales expert Gill Bray, *www.BusinessHat.co.uk*, about this and she chirped in,

❝ I don't believe that most people who say 'networking doesn't work' *deliberately* choose to ignore what they have achieved by networking; they only have one channel open in terms of ROI ie what income have I gained? Their minds are closed to the fact that they have created multiple strands of opportunity, some of which will eventually directly give them income. However, the vast majority will just be 'auxiliary' strands to help them get business e.g. useful information, further contacts, moral support & encouragement, sharing of expertise, goods and services that will aid one's own business. ❞

Fair call Gill, we'll have that, so here's a rundown of some of the things they may well have gained:

INCREASED CONFIDENCE

COLLABORATION

DUE DILIGENCE

FRIENDSHIPS

FREE ADVICE

MARKETING PLATFORM

APPOINTMENTS

MOTIVATION

SUPPLIERS

BETTER PRESENTATION SKILLS

and SALES

See? I put sales right at the bottom, not because they aren't important, they are after all the life-blood of any business, but because sales are a great by-product of all the stuff that precedes them.

Read that through a couple of times again from the *

Do those paragraphs make sense to you?

Honestly, if you believe networking doesn't work, or isn't for you, you're probably coming at it from the wrong angle. Maybe you're taking the vending machine angle or you're in a "business isn't working" period. The problem doesn't lie with the network, but either with you or your offering.

I'm not trying to be critical or negative – it's genuinely not my style – but if you are really serious, as in really serious, about making this magic bullet called networking work, answer the following questions honestly:

1) Does your product rock?
2) Do your customers think it rocks?
3) Is it priced correctly – are you sure?
   Have you sold any?
4) Is your 1-1 appointment approach effective?
5) Is your 40 second pitch good?
6) Are you well-liked?
7) Have you attended regularly?
8) Are you desperate? (Be totally honest)
9) Do you appear to be desperate?

That last question, about being desperate. The sales manager is breathing down your neck, the pressure's on from the 'supportive partner', mortgage payments are due out in three days and you don't have the funds yet? Have your savings or redundancy pay-off dwindled at about the same rate as your enthusiasm?

Then you need to do something, deliver pizzas, whatever,

to keep the wolves from the door. But do something. Anything. Read *GOYA* chapter 2, 'Do Something. Anything', for more on that. Get rid of your desperation, as people smell it, and the powerful, subliminal message is that you are not successful for a reason.

Do you know what?

Networking is rarely a quick fix

It's going to take time. Networking is not a button that you press and out pop orders for your products.

You need to put in a difficult "seemingly making no progress" initial six months, and sometimes even longer, to get the foundations and relationship base on which to build on and go forward. There isn't a single business type where networking doesn't work and yet some people adopt a specific attitude which makes it difficult to gain success from networking.

David Lossl, from *www.thereallyusefulmortgagecompany. co.uk*, is a member who I had memorable 1-1 with at a 4Networking meeting in the cathedral city of Wells. We sat down and it turned out this would have been his final 4Networking meeting if I hadn't spoken with him.

This was no set-up, just a pure fluke. David said that he loved 4N but had had no business from it.

Within ten minutes I changed his mind-set.

Fast-forward a year or so and now 80% of his new and significant £££ business comes from 4Networking.

It's all about your application of the networking. If you come in, as our David did, with a referral mind-set, networking doesn't really work. He was conditioned to focus solely on referrals, referrals, referrals. My suggestion was that he should focus on people, people, people.

His jelly, otherwise known as 'trust' with other members, hadn't set yet.

I'd be lying if I told you I could remember exactly what I said, but that's because I have so many 1-1s with people and end up in ten minutes getting them focused, fired up and on track.

So you, like David, may not be too far off – think of it like looking through a blurred lens of a telescope – a slight adjustment of focus and suddenly there is perfect clarity. You may only be, say, 5-10% off target, but you are still off target.

Remember. This can be fixed in just ten minutes. Perhaps it's already been fixed by the stuff we're talking about in this chapter.

You have to make your mistakes, learn an approach that works for you and so forth – but networking the way I suggest is as close to a magic bullet for business as there is.

So come on, get focused, get fired up, buy into what I'm saying in this chapter. You've bought the book and I'm selling you nothing further!

Although, if you are daft enough to want to give me £16,000 to join my 'exclusive' *Millionaire Mentoring Programme*, ENROL TODAY and you will get a free DVD. On that DVD *I'll share with you THE SECRETS OF INCREASING SALES THROUGH NETWORKING BY 3,428% IN JUST 7 HOURS* ZZZZzzzzzz.

Joking.

Have you ever heard or even said, "Networking eats into my working day"? If you don't consider networking as working, you're right, it's not.

I say to people,

"If you've got something better to do with your time, go do it"

and that applies to any activity you are doing during your day.

Networking IS work, surely? For me it always has been. I sometimes think back to my mind-set in my first year in business. I needed to get to know people and find a route to appointments. Well, networking gave me that.

Primarily, the examples I'll be citing throughout this book are from 4Networking online and offline. To be honest, of course I'm biased about the value of 4N, but generally speaking, wherever you're networking the same rules apply.

As in the gym, you have to be prepared to use a variety of networking equipment to get the maximum benefit. Any decent network will have a number of tools you can use... That means facing up to doing the stuff you don't enjoy because that's probably going to be stuff you are weakest at. And remember, I can't do your press-ups for you, they're down to you.

The route I'm advising is one that makes for rapid growth, but requires six months or so investment of time 'up front' in order to be effective.

At first it may feel as though it's just not working, with nothing quite happening.

But it is.

You are learning more about people, more about your business, more about yourself. Equally, others are learning more about you, more about YOUR business!

This guidance is based on five years of distilled networking experience, on what I've seen, experienced and heard.

Another metaphor for you: when you decide to have a barbecue, you light the coals and wait for 45 mins or so until the exciting-looking flames have gone and you have a constant heat. Effective networking is like that. You can't see flames, but you can feel it, the heat is there.

Schoolboy error, most barbecue 'experts' (er, most blokes)

mistake the wonderfully hypnotic licking of flames as the 'go' sign to begin cooking.

Net result is, twenty minutes later, sausages with cancerous black charcoal on the outside, delightful nicely warmed-up and energetic listeria on the inside... and grief from wifey that she should have done it but, oh no, the barbecue is always boy's territory...

This is similar to being 'sold to' whilst networking. You get talking to someone and they start selling to you straight off; you make the mistake of politely smiling and nodding encouragingly (flames), more out of common courtesy than real enthusiasm for their product and approach.

It's not terribly British to come straight out with a "Really, I'm not interested" and as a result they are now preparing to go in for the kill. Your kill! Ugh.

Net result? You're a burnt networker with a toxic core inside of how you feel about them and, what's more, you're warmed up to spread your toxins by way of warning other networkers about the barbecue merchant.

We've all been there.

You've either tried selling without building trust or have been on the receiving end of one of these flamethrower networking pitches.

Networking contacts, like barbecue coals, have to warm up fully before you can go on to cook. There's a danger that the food may look like it's cooked, but it's in fact cold and poisonous on the inside.

New people often turn up at a networking event and go bang! Zero to sales pitch, instantly.

A total waste of time. B A C K O F F !

To sell more... sell less.

At one particularly corking 4Networking event, at the end of the meeting a first-time visitor ruined the networking value that had built up during the meet by chasing all the other attendees, spending a cursory thirty or so seconds with anyone she could collar, asking the question, "So are you coming to my networking event this Thursday evening?"

You couldn't make it up...

The lady in question ran an independent, tired-old-format business network. She was inviting people by forcing the leaflet for her networking event into the unwilling hands of anyone unlucky enough to be collared by her.

Unbelievable. You're never going to get productive results doing such things. Chasing people around like Benny Hill is never a winning strategy.

Engage, or the answer's "NO"

Pathetic! 4N is receptive to other business networks and lets them in to promote their events, but this was pathetic. The numbers for her events were poor, she was desperate, and it showed. Embarrassing.

Remember,

desperation sells nothing.

Why don't we routinely have problems with group numbers in 4N? I'll tell you why – because people want to come. We have massive re-investment, great processes, great teams and an offering that people want.

So, if you find yourself at a networking event with nine people and start bleating about low numbers, do something about it by changing it to a format that people want or by injecting some genuine energy into proceedings. Beating people over the head with a club to get them to your group for your own reasons rather than theirs is never going to work.

The best way to save money on printing costs when networking is NOT to give your stuff to everyone. If you shove a card, a leaflet or anything else for that matter into my hand, then it will be left on a table or go in a bin. Although since I got a wood burner, I store them up to use as kindling. It's true.

See your second drawer down, you know the one, chock full of harvested business cards?

You are NEVER going to use them for anything sensible. After all, you stay in contact with the people you want to. Do you have a business card for your husband or wife? Nope.

You don't need a business card for someone you want to stay in touch with!

Unless it's a winning lottery ticket, shove something at me without me asking and its going in the fire.

I'm responsible for my actions at networking events. Be responsible for yours.

Ooh! I went on a rant then…

Take this on board. Your priority is not others' priority. People have their own challenges and goals, so therefore going to networking desperate for sales will generally yield you few results. A question I often ask when I do seminars at networking events is: who has come here to buy?

The occasional hand goes up. And yet most people have achieved sales as a direct result of networking activity.

Of course networking has to be about sales: after all we're all in business. However, before you reach that stage, it has to be about meeting people and building relationships. Sales are a by-product of getting people and relationships right, with the last stop on that relationship train being TRUST. Without trust you have no sales.

Let me ask you a question. Would you pass on a lead,

contact, referral, or job to someone you DON'T

LIKE

KNOW

or

TRUST?

Answer is - no, of course not.

Well, how the hell can you expect others to forgo the self-same checks you are doing on them??

"I need bigger businesses" is a classic I hear repeatedly whilst on my travels around the UK. To people who say that, I ask, "Are you a bigger business?" Nine out of ten say they're not. In which case, my reply is, "Piss off then, so the bigger businesses can network".

Our friend feels that he should be the only small business owner allowed to mingle with bigger businesses.

How does that work then?

It doesn't.

Never under- or over-estimate anyone.

Treat everyone the same... with respect.

What's the downside?

More on that in the next chapter.

First and foremost, for networking to work, *you need to have a business that works for you*. You can then build that business using networking and with the option with 4N to network up to four times each week anywhere in the UK and around your schedule, it's never been easier.

When something good happens in your life or business, you get a morale boost. When you get a break, ride the hell out of it – that's what I've always done. I use the energy from even the smallest of victories to carry us onto the next one. I make no apologies for having already mentioned this in *Get Off Your Arse*.

With this book, I'm coming back to some of those lessons, but from a different angle or approach. It's like applying a second coat of paint – it's too valuable a lesson not to repeat.

Not everyone is as nutty and 'out there' as me, you don't have to be, as the principles which run through this book and the cool hints and tips I throw out will work for you.

You just need to apply your own values and slant onto it all.

So, in order to get leads, contacts, referrals and jobs passed to you, you need to be TRUSTED.

The fastest way to build trust is by *being yourself*. However, be aware that in being yourself, the result may be some people NOT liking you.

100% of the time, I am 100% me.

Don't waste your life trying to appease those that don't like you, focus on those that do. When you are in a tribe, don't expect to be winning many friends going into a Liverpool terrace wearing a Man United top.

Accept that not everyone is going to like you. Networking and using social media, like life, is about rolling with those you do get on with – those you find interesting, and in return, find you interesting.

Create fans, not just customers.

People who just love what you do and tell everyone about how fab you are. How do you do that? Provide consistent, excellent service and go the extra mile for people. Then make sure they tell their friends and colleagues about you. Plus, surround yourself with people who support you and your values and believe in what you are doing.

I've had hate campaigns waged about me on the internet. It's the occupational hazard of holding opinions, often strong ones. What should I do? Rush to lawyers to slap 'cease and desist' orders on them? No. It's a waste of time and a waste of energy.

The one flavour in which I'm not available is vanilla, which is one of the reasons I get noticed. It does mean that people sometimes disagree with me. They are entitled to their opinion: buzz-killers and killjoys (as I see them) will always exist.

There are now so many outlets for opinions: twitter, networking forums, blogs. It's great, instead of offending/amazing three of your mates down the pub with your take on the world, you can reach out to thousands with a constant stream of opinions, thoughts and ideas. Get on *http://twitter.com* and you'll see what I mean. Identifying, gathering and building up your tribe has never been easier and it's also just great fun.

So remember, there's only one thing worse than being talked about and that's... not being talked about: ooh, very Oscar Wilde...

Surround yourself with people who support you and your values. Believe in what you are doing. If deep down, you don't believe in what you are doing, go and do something else for a living.

Remember – it's never too late to change direction.

The downside to boxing training:
it might ruin my boyish good looks.

www.evolvetraininguk.co.uk

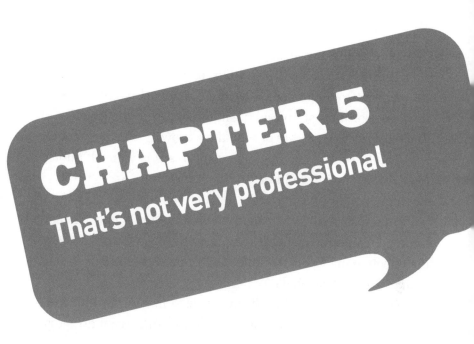

CHAPTER 5
That's not very professional

I'm not as thick as I look, or sound.

A few weeks ago I was walking around a business show. I was doing my usual gig, swanning around in jeans and t-shirt, when I passed a suited-and-booted bloke standing with his mate.

As I walked past he asked his mate, loudly enough to ensure that I heard, "Dress-down Thursday is it?"

I stopped and asked him what he meant. He said "Well. This *is* a business show. You're not dressed very professionally are you?"

"Really?" I asked. "Define 'professionally'", I said.

He couldn't think of an answer.

"Why not come and see how professional I am, as I'm the next seminar speaker up in the 300-seater auditorium?

Although it's oversubscribed so you probably won't get a seat.

Is that professional enough for you?"

Geez.

Don't overestimate anyone. Don't underestimate anyone.

Treat everyone the same. With respect.

Try not to judge people by the car they drive, the clothes they wear or their supposed businesses or experience. You just don't know who they are or who they know!

The last thing you're gonna want to see is yourself quoted in *GOYA3* for being an idiot.

I'm always encountering people in business mistaking being 'professional' as an excuse to be standard, ineffective and boring. I'm about to set you apart from the crowd, with some of the effective marketing techniques I've used. Some may regard them as 'unprofessional'.

Let me ask you this. If, by using some of the following 'unprofessional' tips, you got some new clients, what does that make you?

Lianne Dupre, from D2 Accounting, *www.d2-accounting.co.uk*, had been sending a hundred or so letters to prospects each and every month and getting nowhere fast. Lianne was feeling deflated and discouraged by the whole process and the lack of response.

Then she tried my 'Dear Neighbour' approach and won four new clients in four weeks, who to date she continues to retain!

Coming up next – a way of ensuring your junk mail survives longer than the usual two seconds it takes someone to suss out that it is junk mail before it heads off to its final destination – 'File 13' aka the waste paper bin.

The following 10 tips win attention and help win business. They are worth remembering, especially if you haven't yet beaten four new clients in four weeks!

You ready for them?

The following was taken directly from my blog 'TRICKS YOU CAN PULL TO GET IN FRONT OF SOMEONE', which can be found on *www.getoffyourarse.biz*

More and more, you need to be "noisy to get noticed" in today's business environment. These are some wacky-but-effective tips, Bradfans.

1) **Upside down tip.** Print your letter upside down on the letterhead and send it out. Guaranteed to get a response! Then you speak to them. "You realise you printed it upside down?" they ask.

2) **The 'Dear Neighbour' tip.** Look for prospective businesses within a one mile radius of where you work. No, I'm not going all 'Greenpeace' on you about cutting down emissions through less travel. You contact businesses within that one mile radius target area with a note saying, "As a 'neighbour', I thought it'd be useful if we met. I'm only just down the road". It's a great hook.

3) **The 'Screw Up' tip.** Print your business letter, then write at the top in big marker: "This paper is the only thing we screw up". Then scrunch your business letter up into a ball, tuck it into the corner of an A4 envelope and send it. What would you do if you received this? You'd be curious about the odd-shaped letter, open it, laugh, appreciate the approach and probably even show a colleague or two...

4) **"We can both make money"** tip. Chop a £5 note in half and staple one half to a letter saying, "I'd like to meet up with you so we can both make money".

5) **The pizza tip.** Everyone loves free stuff. I sent piping hot pizzas to journalists in London. They'd open up the pizza box and it had a picture of me in the lid, smiling, winking, holding a pizza box in my hand, together with the words, "There is such a thing as a FREE LUNCH. *WWW.BRADBURTON.BIZ* ". That was

it! That afternoon I got loads of calls and therefore loads of appointments. Send FREE stuff, be it a KitKat, a packet of biscuits, whatever you choose. How great would *you* feel if you received a thoughtful freebie?

6) **The 'dance round your handbag' tip.** Remember the old adage: "You've got to dance around the handbag for a bit before you invite someone back to your place for coffee"? Unless you have a killer offer, resist the urge to sell. Ham-fisted selling switches people off. The only thing you should be selling early on is the opportunity for a phone call or an appointment.

7) **'Nuts on the outside' tip.** Print something on the outside of your business mail that gets attention or at least causes a smile. For example: "LETTER MAY CONTAIN TRACES OF NUTS".

8) **Handwritten tip.** On the subject of letters, try handwriting the envelopes. We experimented with 1,000 printed and 1,000 handwritten envelopes. We had four times more uptake from the handwritten ones.

9) **'Early impact, sell later' tip.** Cardinal rule: your initial approach should aim to create enough of the right impact to secure a ten-minute appointment. That's it. It's not about selling. Some people get caught out with this schoolboy sales error. It's a bit like a CV – its whole purpose is to get you the interview, not the job.

10) **The GOYA tip.**

Stop thinking about it. Stop talking about it. Start doing something about it. Do it. Do it now.

The above are great ideas. Get off your arse, each and every day. Write and send five letters each day. This GOYA approach gives you a sense of direction and purpose.

Hopefully, you can see the tips above for what they are. Being professional isn't about wearing three-piece suits and wielding pocket watches. Nor is being part of the 'professional club' going to do you any favours. Being a business professional is doing the things you need to do in order to keep your business afloat.

Sales letters and emails need to be inviting, otherwise they'll just end up in the bin. You bin sales letters when you receive them, don't you?

Dear Homeowner

Transform your driveway with block paving from Steve Jones Paving.

We're a professional company which has been established since 1976 and the choice has never been greater. Our contemporary blocks or rustic paving – both available in a wide range of designs and colours – cannot fail to enhance your home, whatever its character.

And with 30% discount available on all orders placed during June, individually laid block paving from Steve Jones Paving is more affordable than imitation surfaces.

Our services include supply and installation of paving blocks, kerbs, recessed manhole covers and drainage systems, and the building of walls and steps.

Our professional installations by qualified craftsmen are usually completed in a few days. Site preparation and free debris clearance is included as standard.

We provide a no quibble guarantee on materials and labour. Finance terms are available which include *(contd)* no deposit and nothing whatsoever to repay for up to six months, written details on request.

Contact us now for a free quotation, survey and landscaping advice.

And blah. And blah blah.

ZZZ! A standard sales letter. Where is the innovation? Most firms will say they are "professional". It's a given – so why bother? Sales letters like the one above are better than nothing and, yeah, they do work sometimes. But you are just carpet bombing, with too much wastage.

In today's busy SMS world, people don't have time to read, unless they really want to. So, load up Word and find one of your sales letters.

Take a look at it and think about it. What is its purpose?

Imagine if I were to give you a tenner for every word you can remove from your sales letter whilst retaining its core message.

How much would I owe you?

The next stage is £50 per additional word that can be removed from your newly-edited letter.

See? It really gets you thinking.

Instead of the 175 words in the Steve Jones letter above, I'd go with something like the fifty or so words below:

Dear Brad,

Transform your driveway with SJ Block Paving. All styles available – and with a genuine 30% discount available on all orders placed during June (our quietest time), you won't have to drive a hard bargain.

You'll be relieved to know our paving is better than our puns.

Call 0800 222 2222 and quote 'BADPUN04' for your free survey.

Shake your approach the hell up. One of the things in business I major on is honesty.

For example "and with a genuine 30% discount available on all orders placed during June (our quietest time)": I used this for a client and it worked, because it was a genuine discount and they really did have an empty order book in June. It rang true because it was true.

It's worth thinking about how being honest with clients or prospective clients can work for your business.

So many people are stuck in the past, using old business skills, old business thinking, doing the same old stuff because "that's the way we've always done it."

Some of the older corporate stuff needs to be binned or at the very least revised, to cope with the changes required in this brave new business world.

How about this for an MS Excel propeller head? Instead of tipping up at a networking event as you'd expect, all formal suited-and-booted, Carl Nixon, The Excel Expert, *www.ilovespreadsheets.biz*, is living his brand, prompted by what he read in *GOYA*. Carl is now instantly recognised as the fat bloke wearing a white t-shirt printed with "I Love Spreadsheets". What a talking point! You're hearing about Carl right here! Professional? Who cares? He's getting people talking, which, in a crowded market, is half the battle. Carl has a corking personal brand and it's cost him beans. He has to wear clothes when networking, so why not wear a tee that gets BIG attention?

Other areas that I'm questioning on the "being professional" front are 'initial sales meetings' and writing proposals.

I've been conned in the past. When I ran my first business, a marketing company, I was conned, not maliciously, by spending two hours dicking about at speculative 'sales meetings' whilst giving up the crown jewels of my information. I now have a new motto:

"I'll spend my time when you spend your money".

Anyone that knows me, as in really knows me, is aware that I'm far from uber-hardcore mercenary and will genuinely help anyone. That's my thing. However, giving up my time for a 'fishing trip'? Nah! Count me out. You may also want to apply a similar filter so that you can count yourself out of these capers.

So that's 'sales meetings'.

Now for proposals. Honestly – when you receive a five-page proposal, what's the first thing you do?

I'll bet that 90% of you do what I do and go immediately to the bottom of the last page to see what the £TOTAL is before deciding whether the rest is worth a look.

Therefore I've stopped doing proposals for my 'consultancy' (hate that word – thinking about a better one). I prefer to get a 'feel' for what people are looking for in a conversation. I do this in the first ten minutes. I can then tell them how long I reckon it'll take to get them sorted and how much it'll cost. They can then take it or leave it – right there and then.

The alternative is, and let's be honest, you've probably been there yourself, wasting hours prepping documents only to get a "No", or to find your painfully prepared proposal being used to shave other players' quotes down.

If you must do proposals, create them in a way that lets you reuse them again. You can then just tweak them here and there to personalise them for each recipient.

And definitely don't use proposal writing as an excuse to pretend you're working!

Mike Morrison, from MIMO, *www.mimomedia.co.uk*, told me how during his "being professional" phase he was spending 50-60 hours per month writing 'Initiative Planning Documents' aka IPDs (you couldn't make this stuff up) for his business. This stuff borders on dicking about, but wrap it up in some fancy title and it's called "being professional".

You may well be disagreeing with the above but, be honest with yourself, you've probably found yourself doing this sort of stuff. My hunch is that you might be avoiding doing something that you actually need to do, but which you are finding is much more difficult.

That thing which you're avoiding? Hit it straight on! Yeah, I know it's scary, but 'IPD'ing and holding onto some of the other "being professional" trappings is in fact holding you back from being professional in business.

Back with our friend Mike from MIMO – he also shared with me his story of realising that he was "playing the professional business game" in his first year of business when he shelled out £1,500 for 1000 folders in order to show off when pitching for business. These were wonderful double-sided, laminated, embossed-logo, the lot, folders. Just beautiful! Mike thought he needed these (no doubt with the help of the professional-shiny-folder-salesman) in order to portray a positive, professional image.

I love 'shiny' in business, in terms of presentation. 4Networking was built on this principle. However, as Mike told me,

❝ I didn't really have a purpose for these folders and ended up nursing nine hundred and ninety six of my shiny friends through two house moves before finally loading up my car and taking the remainder to the recycling bin. ❞

Mike's sussed out that what's needed to succeed in his field are not shiny folders: anyone can buy them. Instead it's the ability to develop amazing websites! Good work fella, thanks for sharing your advice, which may mean you, the reader, don't have to shell out 1500 quid for a visit to the recycling centre!

I've done all this stuff as well. When I registered my first company, 4Consultancy, back in 2004, it cost me £129. Fantastic value – especially since I got the wax sealer for any official documents and a brass plaque with my company number for the front of my two-bedroom terraced pad and a load more shite that I didn't need and have never used.

Why? Because I wanted to feel "professional" of course.

For sure, I didn't make that mistake second time around.

4Networking was incorporated for £29 online. Did I want to pay an extra £10 for a "letter of incorporation copy sent through the post"?

No thanks. Ctrl-P'ing of a .pdf will do.

So I saved £100 instantly compared to that first outing. If you extrapolate the cash difference between wanting to look professional compared to being professional over the lifetime of a business, learned from lessons in this book (and others), it could spell the cash difference between success and failure.

Don't confuse "being professional" with repeating the same mistakes that many others make just because they feel good and comfortable or you'll be the skintest professional person. Break the mould.

Make sure you really, really need the shiny thing you're shelling out for to "move your business forward" and that it will move your business forward.

Should you find yourself using terms such as "turnkey solution", ask yourself, "What does that really mean?" It sounds professional enough, though. Right? If you don't know what it means, the chances are you can't use it to "be professional" and it might just be a great alternative label for dicking about.

Since the dawn of business, people have always used "professional" speak, using jargon such as "vertical markets". A great site chock full of more examples like this is *www. buzzwords4u.co.uk.*

Jargon isn't clever and nobody thinks you are clever using it, so try taking it out of your vocabulary and just use normal language that people have a cat's chance of understanding.

Failure to do so may find those words coming back to haunt you in a future GOYA book.

Probably the funniest thing I've read was this absolute peach of business bullshit which I saw with my very own eyes.

It was in a job advert for a major tea company:

"The successful candidate will need to penetrate the customer vertically & horizontally".

What next? Have a fag and a nice cup of tea?

Steer clear of the jargon or people will steer clear of you.

Whilst we're on the subject of avoiding stuff... you have surely come across networking events that are deliberately held at expensive and opulent venues.

What a waste of even more money! Successful networking has absolutely nothing to do with exotic locations overlooking rivers, nor wonderful organic sausages, nor even trips around old whisky distilleries.

Networking is all about the people.

When I see networking events promoted with wonderfully lavish lunch menus at hoity toity venues, I shake my head. I'm not saying that stuff isn't nice, it is. But primarily networking has to be about the people, so to headline with the location is to miss the whole point of it.

Of course it's possible that the venue works for some people, since it allows them to talk about (or even to) the oil paintings instead of themselves. One person who springs to mind as a likely attendee of such an event is the proprietor of a video production company, who I bumped into recently at a trade show.

I said I'd not seen him around lately and he told me that he'd left 4Networking, so I asked him why. I'd noticed that loads of members from the network were working with him and that my understanding was that he had gained at least twenty pieces of business as result of 4Networking, just that I knew of.

This is how he responded:

"I left because I was having so much fun, at times it didn't really feel 'professional' or 'business-like'".

/shakes head

We're not living in Victorian times – you are allowed to enjoy your work, enjoy your networking, enjoy your business. Business life needn't be painful in order to be professional.

I tried the suit-wearing thing recently while speaking at an event. As a result I felt stifled. Constricted. However, if you feel comfortable in a suit and tie – go for it.

I dress the way I do, wear stubble, because it's me. It wasn't always so. Until a few years ago I regularly wore a suit in business: even I felt I should conform for some reason. Since then I've decided to just be myself. I feel much more honest. People know exactly what they're getting from the moment they meet me – or maybe they don't, as the 'dress-down-Thursday' bloke at the tradeshow found out.

Being professional in business isn't about staring all day at spreadsheets, unless of course you happen to be a fat bloke from Wales with a crazy "I love spreadsheets" t-shirt whose name is Carl!

There is no point at all trying to be someone else. If some people don't like you or your style, move on, because others will, and they're the ones you can build trust with.

If you try to be something you're not, you'll be found out in the end.

We leak the truth.

www.ilovespreadsheets.biz

Be different, because different works

I'm really not as thick as I look!

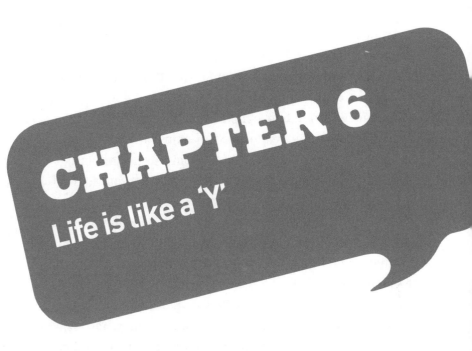

CHAPTER 6
Life is like a 'Y'

We were pretty messed up that night, somewhere in a field. To be precise, we were in a farmyard near a farmhouse in deepest Somerset. This must have been about 1998, a couple of years or so after I moved down from Manchester.

That morning I was with my friend Rik, who worked from home, always had his laptop open "working" and was always starting this or that business. On one occasion, I remember seeing his bank card, a 'Barclays Business' one, on his coffee table. I was quietly impressed, and it got me thinking that like Rik, I'd love to be running my own biz. This idea persisted. The reason I mention this is because at the time of writing I keep recognising certain innocuous things or 'signposts' throughout my life which have stuck, acting like gentle nudges to steer me down my path.

Anyway, back to the farmyard, where the rave was underway. It was about five o'clock in the morning and a hundred or so revellers were still dancing around and the fire-eaters were probably the only people eating anything that night.

We carried a kitchen bench from the farmhouse outside and sat in the garden while the sun came up, with the bass pushing through our bodies at this miniature Glastonbury!

Of all the craziness that evening, there is a particular bit about that night which has risen to the surface. I didn't realise at the time how significant this conversation was until I began reliving that event and began writing this chapter. Little did I know that I'd be living with something that Rik said to me that morning more than a decade later. He said,

❝ Look at this. It's crazy... surreal. You know what? Life is like a 'Y'. We each reach a fork in the road and can go left or right until we reach another 'Y'. We choose left or right again and so on through life. The decisions we make at each of those forks in the road determine who we are and decide what shape our life will be. ❞

Rik is no longer with us. He died a couple of years later at the age of 38 after another night of partying. He suffered a brain haemorrhage. The post mortem stated that he had a problem which could have caused instant death from an embolism at any time during the preceding five years.

This is it, boys and girls.

This is your life.

To my knowledge we only get one, so use it in the best possible way and enjoy your shot at life. In *GOYA* I shared my religion:

Help many. Hurt few. Live life.

I'll never forget Rik; he unknowingly gave me my first murmurings and aspirations of self-employment and the fact that his wise words make it into this book makes me smile.

He was around for the 'Y' in my life where I moved from Manchester into a strange new land of fields and cows and began the transition from hardcore urban party animal to a more sedate and sensible path.

Life IS like a 'Y'! Back in 1997, I was living at the seaside resort of Weston-Super-Mare on the dole. I'd figured that if I had to be low key and unemployed it was better to be low key and unemployed by the seaside.

I half-looked for work, but nothing smacked me in the face until I saw an advert in the job centre. It was for a job as a retail manager at a soon-to-be-opened local computer game shop. The last time I'd had retail experience was eight years before, in 1990, when I worked as an assistant at a... surprise, surprise... computer game shop. Gaming was my primary hobby back then and it still is. I'm a *PlayStation 3* man now.

The company duly mailed me out an application form but, instead of completing it, I left it and left it and left it...for days, before heading it into a wastepaper bin.

Why?

Because my handwriting is untidy and I hated filling out application forms.

The girl I was seeing at the time, unbeknown to me, took the form out of the bin, completed the application and returned it to the company on my behalf.

A week or so later, imagine my surprise when I received a letter from the company, inviting me to an interview for the job as manager.

I went along in a suit borrowed from my best friend Jay,

(see *GOYA* chapter 15) and went for the interview, blah blah blah.

I got the job.

Let's just reverse up a second, because this is so important. My direction and life changed as a direct result of my then girlfriend completing that form. Thank you, M!

Action creates action.

Sitting on your arse (SOYA) wins you nothing, ever.

So the next time you can't be bothered filling in a form or doing something, you are standing at a 'Y' and continuing to just stand there. Do something, anything... choose a definite path at every opportunity and move along.

As I mentioned, I'd been long-term employed since I'd left Manchester. I was depressed, felt totally worthless and this was the first time my life began to change for the better. I had turned the corner. The fork in the road I took in leaving Manchester had brought me to this fork.

I started the job about ten days after the general election in 1997, which became known as the New Labour Landslide. The euphoria at the time felt like the dawning of new hope for the country and new hope for me. A country where I could get off my arse, dust myself off and become something.

I think you could say I was reborn in 1997. This was the beginning of my new life. It had restarted again after a seriously difficult labour.

A different sort of Labour was also born. 'New Labour', which marched triumphantly into 10 Downing Street in the person of Tony Blair, to the chorus of D-Ream's *Things Can Only Get Better...*

My mum and I both stayed at my bedsit that night, watching as Tony Blair gave the 'old politics' a drubbing.

A wave of euphoria swept the nation and, like so many at the time, I was one of those hopefuls, carried along by this new buoyancy. The reason I'm talking about New Labour is this. It would be nine years or so later when we would adopt much of New Labour's approach and bring it to 4Networking, namely the branding, the openness, and even the message that this was a time for change.

I guess in ten years time or so you'll hate me too!

In all fairness some already do, but more about that later...

In political terms, 4Networking would be a refreshing change in the networking field, taking on the old institutions and taking over the middle ground which is where the vast majority of networks should have resided. And yet that was impossible, because prior to us tipping up there was no middle ground. Middle ground networkers had no option other than to go to 'loony left' or 'hard right' networks.

Until we tipped up.

With my struggling first business, pizza-delivering at weekends and whingeing wife, it would have been all too easy to go back to a 'real job' when faced with the 'Y' choice of 'real job' or pushing on with pizza support until I reached another 'Y'.

But I decided against the apparently easier path, choosing to continue walking the clearly more difficult and rocky road.

It's been a slower path, including years of under-investment in terms of relationships and personal income. It's a bit like a slingshot – the more you pull it back, the further it will fly, but back too far and it snaps. Believe you me, our slingshot was as near as can be to snapping on numerous occasions, but we are still here, stronger, bigger and with a greater reach than ever before.

Throughout your life, you are going to be tested. It's like a game of snakes and ladders.

Rapper Jay Z, if his rap music is to be believed, emerged from the ghetto projects of New York, had numerous run-ins with the law and dabbled with drugs and crime.

He made some serious decisions at every 'Y' that presented itself.

This is a guy who now owns a massively successful record company, clothing label and many other investments, is on the *New York Times* Rich List, is now worth $450 million... *and* is married to Beyoncé...

Sometimes you may have to do what it takes to survive and to get past your current situation. That applies to whatever is going on in your life/business right now.

Educate yourself, in whatever you need to know, so you can achieve your goals and ambitions.

You must go on. Never ever give up. Just keep it together... until you reach your next 'Y'.

Remember the innocuous decision you made today? It could well be shaping your future.

Listen to what my friend Gary Gorman, *www.garygorman. co.uk*, has to say about a decision he made some years back when he reached the crossroads:

❝ When I took redundancy from corporate life five years ago I could have got back on the same old roundabout, putting up with the same old 'blah,blah,blah' meetings, with my shiny company car and expense account.

I decided that there had to be a better way... a way that

meant I was captain of my own ship.

Now I've been through some choppy waters and felt a bit seasick at times but what self-employment has given me... beyond (thankfully) a decent living... is the bollocks to tackle anything. Before, I could hide and blame someone else... now there is just me.

That is something I never dreamt I'd get from that decision made in December 2005. **"**

Start saying "Yes" to things.

Great story: Terry Cooper, now Development Director of 4Networking, tipped up at a 4Networking event at the second time of my cold-calling him. Back in 2006 we had eleven groups if I recall correctly. Anyways, Terry turned up at the Portishead 4N launch, joined 4Networking that day and asked if he could set up a group in his town, Clevedon.

Fast forward five years. Terry is now Development Director for 4Networking and has just come back from a successful trip to launch 4Networking in New Zealand and Australia. This marks our first step in taking the 4Networking brand global. And Terry is a part of it.

Think about that! It's just nuts.

All because he said, "Yes". A man who had done a thirty year career in a global corporate organisation, had 'retired', and yet he's now travelling the world developing 4Networking. In Terry's words, he's "having a ball".

I must have been a six year-old when I had a playground fight with another kid, 'Wilko'. I ended up getting the better of the other lad, so I sat on top of him and rained down blows on his head.

I remember coming back home and excitedly and victoriously telling my stepdad, Frank, that I'd won the fight. He instantly slammed me down with a 'frank' and stern talking-to. Fighting is something to be avoided and gloating after a fight was completely inappropriate.

Had I have come home to my real dad that day, who had split from mum shortly after I was born, then he most likely would have congratulated and commended me for beating up Simon Wilkinson.

That was another of those 'Y's in life where someone else would have had the opportunity to steer me down a path, one that would have most likely resulted in a completely different life to the one I star in now.

Interestingly, seven years later at secondary school, I was gloating in front of Simon to the kids in our class about my victory in our first fight. Simon then decided it was his turn to give me a drubbing! My overconfidence as a result of that first tear-up dealt me out an embarrassing and bruising pasting in front of the class. One all.

The lesson here is, even if you stay in the past, the world and the people in it don't.

In order to encourage me to make decisions fast, I've always been one to give myself deadlines. Following another stint of unemployment, life was always a bit stop, start, stop, start. I was massively in debt, with a baby on the way, so I sought out advice from the Citizens Advice Bureau (CAB). They explained my options and suggested that going bankrupt might be the way to go. So I set myself a deadline two months or so into the future.

If I had no job by the deadline, I'd pay the required fee and declare myself bankrupt.

Three days before the deadline was reached, I got myself a job. It was the very job which six short months later I told my employer to shove up his arse before embarking on a path of initially unsuccessful self-employment.

It's clear in retrospect that I was actually unemployable! Too much of a wayward spirit – or something.

So here it is. Make decisions today. Start talking yourself into stuff, not out of stuff. Here is a corking metaphor I use to best describe what it has been like for me and others when starting a business:

Think of starting your own business like being on a trapeze. You have wonderful excitement and enthusiasm, swinging back and forth, back and forth, running your business in those first few months.

It feels so liberating – look everyone, I'm self employed!

Then you have to make decisions, to spend money on networking, marketing, offices or something to move your business forward.

Think of it like jumping from your trapeze to another trapeze.

Not so thrilling now… it's more scary.

The swinging back and forth (dicking about) was OK.

But this is all new… You are uncertain whether to make the jump at all, let alone when to make the jump.

And you wait… and wait… and wait… and before you know it the safety net you had made from enthusiasm, savings and desire has been removed.

The risk and gulf is now even greater, having lost that initial momentum. If only I had jumped earlier you think, and then you start doubting yourself.

As a result, momentum is totally lost… the decision to jump now becomes pretty impossible. You're desperate but you can't let go of your trapeze; instead you hold onto your trapeze even tighter now.

Until the final desperate act, which is having no option but to let go and crash to the ground.

Hopefully the above strikes a chord with you – it's powerful stuff.

Make decisions fast and live with the outcome.

I meet people on my travels who are facing challenges in their businesses. They have spent £thousands on advertising, logos, letterheads and so forth: all great. I hate selling, as you may have picked up, but I love people buying.

I try to advise them as best as I can in brief one-to-one meetings and often suggest that they buy the *GOYA* book, but mostly they ignore that advice. I feel sure that *GOYA* would make a difference and provide answers to many of the questions they are asking.

The crazy thing is these people who choose not to do so will continue to haemorrhage further cash because they want things just to magic themselves right. They can't be bothered to read a £13 book which provides the answers to so many of their challenges. But they would prefer to spend £299 to attend a seminar with me which simply covers the same stuff as in the £13 book (damn, given away my secret...)

Passive magic. No one can do your press-ups for you: if you can't be bothered to read a book which gives you guidance then you are set to fail. Naturally that doesn't apply to you. Why? You're reading this, aren't you?

Why are you reading this? Because you want to make changes, need a different direction or approach and reading this will help you to form a new way and find fresh ideas.

Those that choose not to will be sitting ducks for dream-weavers to come along and fleece them. The difference between a £13 book and a £299 seminar (apart from 286 quid) is that someone stands in front of you for £299.

The way things are packaged makes all the difference.

If you are there now, you've reached that 'Y' in the road. So I suggest, like our Terry, you start talking yourself into things.

Like 4Networker Jane Snee, *www.businessdataprospects. com*, who shared with me her story:

"I don't believe there are any wrong decisions in life; all are right decisions and some have learning curves which lead us to different places...

Only a few years ago, I had a great job, corporate company, excellent salary – blah blah blah but I felt so empty inside. I eventually walked and this last 12-18 months has been amazing, every day is totally different.

To think I was told a hundred times I would regret leaving my career. The main thing I have learnt is to listen to yourself, always do what feels right for you – other people's opinions are quite often their own fears, not yours."

Remember – a mistake is only a mistake AFTER the event:

up until that point it's the correct decision.

At times throughout my journey, I've also been scared as hell to make decisions. The reason my life changed for the better was that I chose to make decisions: right or wrong, I just made them. You have more chance of moving up the ladders on your snakes and ladders board if you throw the dice instead of waiting for the dice to roll themselves.

You have a decision to make right now, 'Y', because you have to decide - if you want to move forward...

Why wait? What are you waiting for?

For fork's sakes, take one!

CHAPTER 7
Speed & innovation smashes old & stagnant EVERY TIME

Adapt or die.

"I have no time for social media, it's a total waste of time", he said as he sat in his box room aggressively waiting for his phone to ring.

Me? I just LOVE Twitter. It's arguably the best free business/networking tool in the world and you should love it too.

Think of it like a conversation that is going to happen, whether you are there or not.

Social media expert, and he really is, Stefan Thomas (*www.noredbraces.co.uk*) said to me during a meeting,

〰〰〰〰〰〰〰〰〰〰〰〰〰〰〰〰〰〰〰

❝ The last time I checked, there were more people on the internet on a Sunday evening who can help my business than sat in their living rooms watching repeats of *You've Been Framed*. ❞

It's just like talking in real life, but on a computer. Don't confuse it as something radically different to what you've continued to do since being a child: you know, that stuff called communicating, associating with those people you want to and avoiding the ones you don't.

That's what you do in life: social media is no different. To over-engineer it is to misunderstand it.

Get on this whole social media thing, why? Because kids, your competitors are, so it's a case of moving with the times. Failure to embrace change, in terms of what's happening in the market place or indeed upstairs /*taps forehead* will see you left behind. A couple of people I follow on Twitter and who write blogs on social media that I regularly visit and rate highly are *@WarrenCass www.warrencass.com* and Rebecca Hollis *@BeckySocial www.socialgeekiness.com*. Do yourself a favour and check them out.

If you are not on this bandwagon right now, there IS still time. You need new technology, new ideas, because speed and innovation smashes old and stagnant EVERY TIME.

Here's a great example of that – for years I've been a Sky+ convert; I'd always wait until a film hit Sky Movies, avoiding all that palaver and expense of visiting the cinema.

That was until I was coaxed back to the cinema by the blockbuster *Avatar*. Initially I'd ignored it, nah, not for me for the reasons above, but then the buzz started building and building... and bloody building. People talked not only about this magical film, but also about the amazing graphics and how they were moved to tears and enthralled by the action.

Then to top it all off, the new 3D technology was what bacon is to any good dish, it just makes it better. The 3D just had to be seen. This was going to change the cinematic experience forever.

WOW.

It was just a matter of time now, as I had been hit and sold from multiple angles. My resistance was ground down and I have to say, yes, that

11 foot female blue alien chick IS hot... and fellas, yes, I would.

Ahem.

There are several strands to this story…

So there I am standing in Cineworld in Bury St Edmunds in East Anglia. It was about seven quid for the standard seat, but sod it, that big spacious, comfy luxury seat had my name written all over it, after all I deserve a treat, I've been working really hard and it's been a long time since I last visited the cinema, plus what's an extra few quid for the 3D version and the glasses?

By the time I bunged on some buttered popcorn and a Pepsi, I'm in for £20+.

So there I am at 8pm, watching the trailers, chomping on my sugar popcorn: I'm always torn when faced with the salt/ sugar popcorn thing, but that's a whole chapter in itself.

So I begin tweeting, sharing with my 3,000 Twitter followers how excited I am to be seeing the film that everyone's talking about. Next thing, in my timeline appears this:

@Cineworld @BradBurton we're delighted you like our cinema & seats & hope u enjoy the film, but we'd appreciate it if you'd put your phone away!

I couldn't believe it, I responded with a tweet:

@Cineworld Oops sorry /sits on naughty step

And turned the phone off immediately.

Interesting: James Cameron the director went $70 million over his initial $237m budget with *Avatar* and was rapidly losing the support of the studio and his financial backers. I remember hearing a radio interview where some pundit was taking potshots at Cameron on the eve of *Avatar*'s premiere.

However it then went on to be the highest grossing movie of all time with $2 billion generated from box office revenues alone.

Put that in your pipe negheads.

For any pioneer, the line between massive success and massive failure is often a close one.

During the movie I cried 3 times by the way, I'm such a soft arse. I was however comforted by a family box of *Maltesers* but please don't let anyone know about that, I'd hate people to know I was scoffing malt based chocolate instead of a manly *Yorkie*.

After the film, which was just as everyone had said, magical, awesome and full of innovation, I re-tweeted (RT) @*Cineworld*'s tweet to my followers and guess what, they RT'd it onwards.

A real person representing a business at the end of the computer...

At eight in the evening, I don't know why I didn't expect a real person to be there, engaging with me online, but the lesson is clear: the internet is all about people, not computers, people.

The same goes for business networking: it's nothing to do with business, it's all to do with people.

So why is it that people take a whole different approach online? After all you wouldn't walk straight up to someone and go from nought to sales pitch? Well I'd hope not immediately, yet people do just that on this new fangled medium called the internet.

There are whole industries being built on 'social media' but still, I'm always sceptical of the

'SECRETS OF TWITTER REVEALED'.

Over-complicated solutions to what effectively is just·

communication. Do you have a SMS text messaging strategy?

For me, here's the secret of Twitter, all in less than the 140 character limit for a single Twitter message:

Be yourself and say interesting stuff.

There, I've still got over 100 characters left AND I've just saved you £99 and a day out of the office.

In being yourself you will gain and lose followers, but isn't that what life's about? What the hell's the point in listening to conversations that don't interest you?

That's the reality of Twitter: as long as you are gaining more followers than you are losing, that's got to be a positive.

Somebody took it upon themselves to point out to some 4Networkers that my 'professionalism' was in question, as they took the trouble to count up 126 instances of me swearing on Twitter. OK, guilty as charged, but generally this is late at night at weekends and there may have been alcohol involved. See for yourself by visiting the tongue-in-cheek web-based utility *www. cursebird.com*. Tap in *@bradburton* where last time I looked it described me as an

"enthusiastic pornstar".

I quite like that.

Now you may say there is no place in business for swearing, but a couple of things before you or any other members of the Mary Whitehouse internet police say, "Quick! Let's switch off the internet".

It's my personal account, where I share my life and promote my business interests.

At the time of writing I've sent 26,768 tweets. To put this in context, Stef Thomas has sent 9,655 tweets and he started on Twitter 6 months before me.

I can't be bothered to work out my non-sweary to sweary

tweets ratio because it's really not important, but be aware that some people can and will try to use your social media footprint against you. There's no eraser on the net, once something is out there, it's there for good…

These complaints feel a little bit like those who scour the adult Sky channels late at night and then pen a 3 page protest letter to Sky about the "filth" being pushed into their living rooms. Not of course, you understand, that I've ever watched *Babe Station* on Sky Channel 906…

Anyways, I'm on a ramble, but don't be put off by the occasional social media horror story. Accept that not everyone is going to agree with what and how you say stuff. In fact, embrace disagreement. At least it means you're being noticed and that your tweets are being read! Being vanilla on Twitter sucks: spark debate, annoyance, controversy, admiration, frustration, anything but indifference! And above all, be yourself. The strain of tweeting 26,768 times in some sort of voice that was different from the real Brad Burton would have killed me…

Think of it this way: as with networking,

if you feel the need to take a piece of squared paper, a calculator and pencil to try to work out the ROI on your social media activity, it's probably not for you.

The key thing is to enjoy it. It should never be just a box ticking exercise. If you treat it just as that, your Twitter account statistics will look as dismal as this: "71 tweets, Following 458,

Followed by 42, last tweet May 2009"…

I follow about 300 or so people, all of whom I really engage with. I have a frequent, ongoing dialogue with them. I'm massively active on there, but I struggle to keep up with juggling just that number.

Some people are following 10,000. Are they for real?

They are using this new internet as if it's the old one. Back in the olden days of the internet, way back in say 1999, when it was all about broadcast, carpet bomb: hey, you can reach the whole world, so let's literally try to do that.

Now, for those that get it, it's more about a 2-way conversation, dialogue, engagement…

I saw a seminar where a Social Media Expert (in his own head anyway) said that it's "bad manners" not to follow everyone who follows you on Twitter: these clowns are selling SM services as hard gospel. Scary.

Anyways, enough about Twitter. As you can probably tell I'm a big fan, and if you are interested in seeing what all the hoo-haa is about, please track me down and introduce yourself at *http://twitter.com/BradBurton*

It would be impossible to do a chapter on innovation without mentioning the *iPad*: what a game changer.

There are now two types of people in this world, those with *iPads* and liars.

You see those smug *iPad* bastards on the train, you just know they are stealth bragging, smirking at your puny netbook. */shakes fist…*

I'm a total gadget-head but I've managed to avoid buying

one… yet. Once V2 drops, I'm all over it. I'm now on an inevitable *iPad* conveyor belt: just like the movie *Avatar 3D*, it's only a matter of time. One new killer application or upgrade, one smug commuter on a train journey too many and I'll buckle and get one. I'll then have smugness *Top Trumps*: "Ah, yours isn't the new gazillion capacity version, shame…"

What's stopping you creating hype about your products, your business, getting people talking? I call it having a conversational strategy: 4Networking has built up a real head of steam now that it is a truly national network. People are talking about us online and off, mostly positively, which is of course preferable, but negatively sometimes too. That's OK, because "any publicity is good publicity". There's a constant stream of comment about every aspect of the 4Networking experience on our own *www.4networking.biz* community but also on other forums, on blogs, on Twitter, all over the place.

Bring it on!

Occasionally, in response to a posting on the 4N forum, some template legal letter lands on my desk, asking us to remove X post, saying it's defamatory blah blah. How much better, rather than this old school approach, to use the forum platform as an opportunity to answer your critics and gain some respect, rather than scuttling off to the lawyers?

Occasionally you will get people having pops at you regardless of whether you are listening or not, we'll get to that in Chapter 10.

If you do a great job, providing great and innovative products/services, others will do your marketing for you, because your customers become your fans.

Blam! That's it, you need to turn customers into fans, but how do you do that?

While we can't all think of *iPads*, we can all be different, because ultimately that's all innovation is, something different.

I just love what Tref Griffiths of *www.customerlogic.net* has to say on this subject.

---

66 Innovation always wins in the end and it's much easier for a small business to innovate than bigger companies. Smaller businesses have nothing to lose, no reputation to keep up and no shareholders to please.

Time and time again we see smaller, innovative companies come along, steal the market and win massively:

Maxwell House should have been Starbucks, but they didn't see the opportunity.

Barclaycard should have been PayPal, but they were afraid to try a new way of working.

Sotheby's should have been Ebay, but they ignored the online market.

Small businesses have a massive advantage when it comes to innovating, and it just takes one person with a bit of bravery and some creativity to change any market forever. 99

Bang on! See, I was a staunch *ITV News* viewer until *Sky News* came along with faster, sharper and leaner news coverage. I no longer view *ITV News*, but I've converted from a passive news viewer into a massive fan, an advocate of *Sky News*. Rupert Murdoch doesn't pay me to tell everyone how much I like his channels. But I do anyways.

I don't know if Dyson vacuums up better than any other 'hoover' but what I do know is they look funky as hell. Speaking of 'hoovers', the loveable *Henry* is effectively just 2 stickers for eyes. That's the major difference as I see it and all of a sudden you have a new brand. Something people are talking about.

I came up with an idea for my local gym – to rent out free DVDs to all members, with a twist: each visit, you can borrow a movie, and if you bring it back the next day, it's free. Bring it back the day after and it costs £2. This is a total no-lose gamble, paid for by members using the gym more, spending more money while they are there, or coming back a day late. The gym found, for example, that *Avatar* only needed 6 rentals to break even. For the gym it was a unique selling point and everyone started talking about it.

Everyone.

To get people talking about your brand, you don't need a massive budget: you just need some great ideas.

Another example of this is Matt Purser from Longcroft Cat Hotel, who has set up a 5 star hotel cattery. Instead of being a bog standard £11 a night cattery, it's fitted it out like a 5 star hotel: big plush cushions, wallpaper, little mini beds. It's completely nuts and OTT, the kind of thing you expect to see in Beverly Hills, not... Hertford.

This crazy idea ended up being featured in all the major daily newspapers, with the cherry on the cake being on the *And*

Finally slot on ITV's *News at Ten*.

A supposedly daft idea ended up attracting hundreds of thousands of pounds of media exposure because it was innovative and different.

It's changed the UK cattery game forever, see for yourself at *www.longcroftcathotel.co.uk*.

People are talking about it, geez, even I'm falling for it by telling you.

Coupled with innovation, you need speed of implementation too, to maximise your advantage.

You have to find a way to create shock and awe in your audience: *Avatar* and *iPad* have achieved it, but so has our friend Carl from the previous chapter, the difference being he did it with £zero budget.

You can do the same... think... think... think...

...of a way to hit your audience from multiple angles to get them to sit up and take notice, and then, even more importantly, to get them to make *their* contacts take notice.

It does need to be genuine innovation though. All the time, we see people lifting bits from 4Networking and cobbling something together, pretending that it's new and fresh. We have proven that we have a perfectly good racehorse, but if you try to stick a couple of humps on it, it becomes a camel.

The era of the friendly bank manager who likes to say "Yes" and is the small business owner's friend has ended.

The greedy financial institutions have closed down that

channel of support: the suits are still in business, they just ain't lending to the likes of you or me.

Having been bailed out, they now prefer to say "No".

Our bank doesn't issue current account business debit cards (nuts, I know), so we wanted to move from a £2,500 to a £3,000 monthly limit on our company credit card. This was to allow for the wider geography of the network, more nights away in hotels and just general business growth.

It was getting embarrassing to get an 'Authorisation Declined' two days before the end of the month, having reached the credit limit on our company credit card.

So I put a call in to the Senior Business Manager, get his answering machine and 36 hours later pick up a voicemail which said something like:

"We'll need to have up-to-date 3 year accounts to increase the limit by £500".

Honestly, we'd never been overdrawn, had increasing turnover and growth and had always paid the £limit each month, so the increased risk was £500 on a business turning well over £1 million a year.

You couldn't make it up! A busy and growing business had to dish up 3 years of accounts in order to get an additional 500 quid on a credit card. Count us out.

I rang him back and asked, "Would you like the shirt off my back and to set a date when you can sleep with my wife?"

He found it about as funny as I found his request. All

over £500 ffs.

If a 'Senior Business Manager' can't make an informed judgment or genuinely requires 3 years' accounts just to increase slightly a company credit card limit then there is no hope for any of us. I'll talk about it later. There is no cavalry, it's all down to you, as their job (the banks/tender processes) seems to be to waste your time.

Bankers spend all their money chasing 'switchers' and bringing in new business. My advice to you bankers: existing business is just as important as new business.

We had reached a fork in the road, where we could choose to walk the path of being messed about or one where it was time to change direction and change our bank. So we closed the account down and changed banks.

Don't slow your business down with unnecessary rules.

What's that?

You enjoyed the banking story in this chapter so much that you want another example of corporate stupidity?

No probs, coming right up!

There's this massive budget hotel chain, spending big money on a TV campaign, yet the reality didn't match the ads.

We had a Hotel Account Card with a £1,000 limit per month and used it to pay on time, every time. This worked beautifully for about 6 months, until one of 4N's directors tried to book a hotel with it.

"I'm afraid that card is no longer valid", said the woman on reservations. "Sorry, yes it's been withdrawn, you should have received a letter about it."

"No", says us, "OK, we will get another one issued."

A letter arrives, and it goes something like this:

Dear customer, our insurers have removed accounts which are no longer blah blah blah.

Effectively the hotel chain was saying that we were no longer the kind of customer they wanted.

UNBELIEVABLE! No idea how they came to that conclusion. Why spend millions of pounds chasing new business only to turn away a loyal customer who is growing and who always pays their bills on time?

Just madness.

You've probably got your own examples of the computer saying "No". Think about the massive damage to a brand of turning away paying customers. It's not just lost revenue, but lost reputation and credibility too, particularly with so many opportunities to burn these companies on Twitter etc.

I wonder if a director of that budget hotel group would have taken the same view? We'll never know, as regardless, these people and actions represented the organisation, the ethos, the culture and for me they've blown it. Every bit of goodwill and brand equity. Finished in an instant.

Can you see the opportunity? This is now the time for you to capitalise on the big corporates' stupidity, their fumbling of their own ball.

Recently, for the first time in 4Networking's five year history, I came up with something that, although it would probably have made the member experience better, implementing it would have created mayhem. With so many things that would have required to be changed right across the UK network, the upheaval outweighed the benefit. Training videos would have had to be re-shot and edited, printed literature scrapped and so forth.

I realised that we've changed from a speedboat to the tanker. From the early days, when there were no processes, just action, we have now become increasingly process driven. But what we've got now is hopefully a format and an ethos which will carry us forward for the next few years.

So when you are fleet of foot and have no money, when all you have is enthusiasm, ideas and explosiveness, remember that one day you may well still have them, but they can no longer be deployed in the same ways you once did. Interesting times.

In those early years, worry about processes AFTER you've stopped worrying about sales.

See, now is your time, armed just with your laptop in your spare room, to come out swinging and make a dent on the entire UK business scene. It can be done, look at 4Networking: no investment, no bank loan, just innovation, genuine belief, passion in what we were doing, plus a shed load of hours' work and a willingness to make calls, lots of them extremely fast. On top of all that, an embracing of social networking because we enjoy it, not because of the business benefits.

The suit and tie brigade are old money. Like a proliferation of 'new money' there's a new culture in business built not on flash offices and double Windsor knots, but built on people.

In this new economy your capability is judged on whether you can you do it rather than what certificate you hold or whether you should be able to do it because your parents spent a fortune on your education.

You can do this you know. Whatever weird and wonderful ideas you've got going on upstairs, they are doable. Listen, the fact that you are reading this book means you are committed to making your dreams happen.

A journalist for a national newspaper interviewed me and was really getting stuck in, asking some heavyweight questions. She thought she had me cornered when she asked,

"Are you saying other business networks don't work?"

No, I'm saying colour telly beats black and white every time.

To re-state that blinding Tamsen Garrie-ism,

The boss says "Go".

The leader says "Let's go".

This is a message to you the reader...

Speed, innovation...

Let's go.

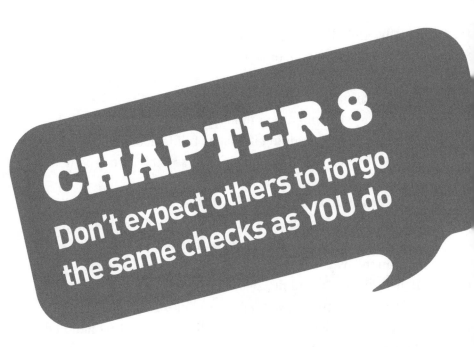

CHAPTER 8
Don't expect others to forgo the same checks as YOU do

et me ask you a couple of questions...

What's the difference between email marketing and spam?

You send email marketing,
the recipient gets spam.

What's the difference between direct mail and junk mail?

You send direct mail, the recipient gets junk mail.

Hopefully I've made my point.

The companies you are targeting pay people and use systems to stop you getting through to them. Receptionists and PAs will bin your mail, spam filters will block your emails.

And guess what, I've got them all too! Receptionists, PAs,

firewalls, junk filters... even battleaxes!

At some point you, or someone you know, has spent hours crafting a wonderfully worded prospecting email to 'key decision makers' like me and 'lifted' an email list from somewhere in order to carpet bomb a few thousand lucky recipients. I'll bet they felt really clever doing it, just as I did back in 2006, when I blasted the hell out of my email lists, as back then it actually seemed a good use of my time.

In the vast majority of cases, with the carpet bomb approach to email marketing all you get back is "address not found" rebounds, complaints about spamming and the privilege of being binned by your service provider, all of which can leave you deflated, disturbed and puzzled by the total lack of response.

Hang on, I spent days drafting and preparing that email.

I remember having to ring the US call centre that handled my email marketing and put on my best Hugh Grant voice to explain why I had so many complaints and unsubscribes. I got away with it for a short amount of time...

before being blacklisted by ALL the email marketing platform providers.

I do mean ALL.

Oops.

But everything's changed now: I reckon that email marketing is yesterday's man. I now add all email marketing to BLOCKED SENDERS. The internet's gone two-way, it's no longer any use as a medium for broadcasting. Now you should use the internet as a vehicle to engage people.

Engage people in dialogue, in conversation.

Do it for 2 reasons

1)   You enjoy it.

2)   Not to sell, but to engage

As with any use of technology or marketing, ask yourself this question:

Would it work on you, as in... would it *really* work on you?

Would you read, respond or just delete your own email as soon as it hit your Outlook?

That tweet you just sent, would you respond to it positively or just ignore it?

A contributing factor to our massive growth is that I apply this question to every element of our external marketing, social media and message.

I put myself into the mindset of my target audience, as in right into it. I always ask myself, will this piece of activity work? Would I respond?

Take a minute to think about all your activity: does it work, not just for you, but, putting yourself in the shoes of your potential punters, is it likely to get a response or just be binned?

A friend of mine was looking for a new car and talked about the extras you can buy. Apparently, for an extra £1800, you can have heated front/rear windows and heated front/rear seats. Hang on, just short of two grand for that??

The salesman at the dealer, he's clever, he doesn't call it that: he refers to it as a *Fully-Loaded Winter Pack* and suddenly you have something you want to talk to your friends about over the dinner party table. "Remember last winter? Well I just bought a new 4x4 Range Rover *Sport*, fully-loaded – it's even got the *Winter Pack* to ensure I can get around". The reaction has changed from "How much??" to "That sounds worth having".

Do that with your business: productise your services, give people something to be proud of, something they can talk about to others.

Back to the *iPad*… yeah, you're paying for the hardware and you're paying a premium for adopting early, but if you're honest doesn't it feel just a little bit good being on the receiving end of those envious other commuters on the train who are thinking "Look at that smug bastard!"?

See what I did there…?

With some thought, you can transform something that isn't working into something that does: it's never too late to change direction.

A guy recently tried to flog me some property or other in Barbados, really not my thing as I can't stand sandy beach holidayZZZ.

Anyways, he's fully into his pitch and forces his business card into my hand, for me to put straight into my back pocket to be binned as soon as I pass one. It gets worse: his card is one of those self-printed ones from a business card making kit. I recognise it straightaway, because I used the same kit back in 2004: nasty threads of cardboard from the serration, horrid. False economy.

The guy is telling me that I'm going to make loads of money on this property, yet he's got a business card that screams, "I'm on my arse".

Another time, I got a phone call from an unrecognised number, "Hi Brad, it's John."

John who?

"John X, you know, from the Office Company over in South Wales, long time no speak, how are you?"

The reason it was long time no speak is that this person had left 4N 3 years before, preferring another business network. Absolutely fine, but let's not pretend to be bezzy mates, having had no communication for years.

"I'm good, what can I do you for?"

"Erm, Brad you're a man that's connected and knows lots of people and

I've got this opportunity where you can make £27,000 each month!" he said excitedly.

"WOW"

"Yeah, it's these properties in Cyprus blah blah blah."

"John, I'll stop you there, are you making £27k per month?"

"No, not yet, but I will be."

"I'll tell you what, give me a call when you are, as I'm a bit busy right now walking my Labradoodle".

*click

If this had been a face-to-face conversation, he'd have had a face like a dropped pie at this point.

Unless you're a character in a soap opera, you can't just walk back into someone's life after having been away for so long and expect to be right back in the TRUST zone.

It's lazy, it's mercenary and it doesn't work. Not in my world anyways.

Don't forgo those vital checks. Now if it had been someone I'd known and had constant contact with over those three years, I'd have been more receptive to listening. It would probably still have been a "No". But I'd have listened.

It goes back to this whole 'Meet, Like, Know & Trust' thing.

People BEFORE business, every time.

John tried putting business before people and guess what?

He came up empty.

Relationships with people are like getting into a hot bath. You need to lower yourself in gently and then once you're immersed you wonder what the big deal about getting in was.

Jump in too fast and bang, you are straight back out, back to square one.

Occasionally callers to our 4Networking Helpdesk ask, "Can you tell me the types of people and businesses that attend your networking events?"

NO, we can't. Why? Does it matter?

It's back to the whole thing about networking. Forget about the job title on the card, YOU are a whole lot deeper than your current role: you have contacts and experiences which have built up across your entire life.

"I need bigger businesses" is another point people keep making. I fire back the question, "Are you a bigger business?"

9 times out of 10 they answer…

NO

"Well in which case can you piss off and allow the bigger businesses to network!"

It wouldn't be much of a networking event on that basis.

Look, everyone knows BIGGER BUSINESSES. We each have a friend or relative, a contact who has clout within these 'mythical' larger organisations, so it stands to reason that those people you encounter do as well.

Let's be realistic: is the BIGGER BUSINESS'S sales executive that you meet whilst networking likely to get you in front of the MD? Nope, they are preoccupied with selling in order to keep their job. Yes, you are possibly one step closer, but it's unrealistic. I'm not saying don't bother at all as that goes against the whole ethos of networking. However my point is that good leads often come from the least obvious of places and people.

Forget about the FTSE 100 company logo on someone's card:

it's nigh on irrelevant if they don't LIKE you.

I don't want to keep banging the nail in, but if we all start to appreciate that everyone has value and worth, the biz world will be a better place for it.

It's likely that all those people you have come across in life are much deeper than may first appear and it's up to you to uncover what lies beneath those layers.

Having said that, there are times when the lack of chemistry is insurmountable. I once had a ten minute 1-1 with a guy at a meeting, which felt like an eternity. After two minutes, we ran out of things to say: it was clearly the world's worst fit ever. We just stared blankly at each other and after 90 seconds or so of this, I said "I'm gonna go and have a look at the bumf table."

Bad fits in life and business are always going to happen. The difference in this case was at least I'd not spent £30 on fuel and wasted 90 minutes of my life driving just to have a meeting that was never going to work.

In life, it's the good fits you're looking for and here's one I love:

There's a bloke in Weston-Super-Mare who runs a back street garage called JB Autos. I've used him for well over 10 years. He's seen me drive all manner of cars in that time, including the M-reg Vauxhall *Omega* with rust on one wing which powered me through those first couple of years of self-employment.

Garage John, that's my name for him, took my wifey's car in for a new radiator. I estimated it at £200 or so. He rings me to say it's fixed; I go back to collect the car and when I ask how much I owe him, he says, a tenner!

Erm... I thought it needed a new radiator?

Nah, I fixed it with a bottle of this (glass repair liquid) or something.

It's fine.

Now I'm telling everyone about Garage John. We ALL do that, you do that.

You get good service, you tell everyone, you get bad service, you tell everyone.

Funny little fact about Garage John which backs up what I just talked about. He was the bassist in Edison Lighthouse, the '70s band behind the #1 chart hit, *Love Grows (Where My Rosemary Goes)*. People really are deeper than the title on their business card.

The key to success in your business is to get everyone talking about you. Positively is better than negatively, but sometimes even negatively works, if you can handle it.

I've just come off the *Jeremy Vine Show* on Radio 2, where I'm a regular contributor. This time out, I was debating whether or not putting flyers under windscreens is a legitimate marketing tool for businesses or a pain in the arse. My view is it is both. Google the clip, I'm sure you'll find it.

Having kicked off 4Networking back in 2006 by doing just this, my point of view was that it has its place if done correctly...

Back then, I'd get up at 6am and make my way to a competitor's breakfast meet, as I knew what time they would sit down and what time they'd finish the meeting and return to their cars.

I'd start at the front of the venue and snake my way back to the vehicles at the rear of the car park, flyering all of them about 4Networking before jumping in my trusty 'n' rusty M-reg Vauxhall *Omega* whose engine I'd kept running.

It was like a military operation. I'd get a wonderful rush of adrenalin each time I did it, truly thrilling. I'd do whatever it took to build momentum for 4N in those first few months.

'Visitor Days' were like shooting fish in a barrel, as people would return to their cars and have an envelope under their windscreen.

The envelope read: GOOD MORNING?

What would you do if you had a sealed envelope under your windscreen? You'd open it!

It created absolute uproar. Brill!

Everyone was talking about it, some positively – ooh that's clever.

Some negatively – who the hell do these 4Networking people think they are?

I have an uncanny ability to wind people up in a marketing capacity.

We then had people coming along to see what all the fuss was about. They'd come along determined to hate it, but find themselves seeing that this really was something fresh and different in networking.

People migrated from other networks in their droves. It was a networking exodus the likes of which the UK hadn't seen before.

Positively and negatively, people were talking – it turned out to be the kindling that set off a networking bushfire that would engulf the entire country.

I now walk around doing seminars in jeans, t-shirt and trainers, why? Because it's more 'me'.

For me, it's this season's 3-piece suit. Why conform? Who the hell are you doing it for? Break the mould, be unique, be different to your competitors, otherwise it comes down to price.

Being authentic means you are being you, lowering your guard, and if people take advantage of that, it's a great way of them deselecting themselves fast. Best we find out early doors.

Mike Morrison from MIMO came out with yet another blinder: he said that the only thing wearing a suit in business proves is that you know how to buy a suit.

I do like that.

What do you do when someone forces their business card into your hand? Honestly, with me it goes straight into my back pocket, its first stop on a journey to the wood burner.

I've started handing cards back, saying thanks but I won't use it. Now either I'm being rude or being brutally honest, but at least I'm doing my bit to save the environment.

If someone asks for your card, by all means give it to them and then engage, talk, communicate, otherwise it's the nightclub equivalent of giving a bird the wrong number.

More and more cards at networking are being used to create ineffective spam lists. There are no shortcuts anymore and the new school way of doing business is with people you like.

This stuff may sound a bit radical, but I'd go on record as saying that no one has done as much breakfast networking as me over the last 5 years, so I know what I'm talking about. Oh yes, and it's no accident that I'm this fat.

Boom boom. Was that joke any funnier 2nd time out?

A few years back, I received a snotty message via the 4N Helpdesk from a woman who demanded that I return her call

so I gave her a bell. She answered and explained that she was head of fundraising for a charity and had visited 4Networking three times as a visitor and was dismayed when one of the 4N team told her that she would have to pay and join 4Networking in order to attend more meetings.

Her view was that as part of our Corporate Social Responsibility we should give her and the charity she was employed by a free membership. It turned out that her "charity" was a £2 million pound sailing ship which took disabled children on one day excursions.

All very noble.

It seemed to me that the charity was more about paying for the upkeep of the owner's tall ship rather than helping disabled children. So the call continued like this:

I suggested that she sell the boat and with the £2 million raised, charter another ship for the 60 or so active days per year that they organised excursions. I then asked her if she was paid more than £30k a year to raise funds for the charity and she said yes, she was. I explained that this was about £15k more than me and suggested that if she felt so strongly about the charity, she should pay for the 4N membership out of her own money.

/click

It's not that I'm unsympathetic to charities: we do a hell of a lot for the 80 or so we now support in each area up and down the UK. We have something called fun fines: if somebody's mobile phone goes off, it's £1, unfunny heckling is £1, with all fines given to the 4N Area Leader's nominated charity.

What I'm unsympathetic about is piss-takers who use the cover of a charity for their own ends.

She wasn't prepared to pay for a networking membership out of her own wages, yet wanted us to take it out of ours. A woman who didn't know me expected me to do something that she wasn't prepared to do. How does that work?

It doesn't.

Hopefully this chapter will help you to question those things you are doing with your business/life. Question whether they really are effective or are they just things you've always done because it feels safe? We are creatures of habit and change is often associated with difficult. But if things aren't working how you would like them to, maybe that's because you are expecting people to forego the same checks that you are doing.

Think about that...

CHAPTER 9
Insufficient funds

AUTHORISATION DECLINED

It's happened to me on more than one occasion over the history of running 4Networking.

Being an MD is all about:

Private number plates, spinny chairs, company credit cards and BMW *5 Series...*

Isn't it?

Well, maybe a few years down the line, but in those formative years it's more about being frog-marched over to cash machines... as happened one evening when I was out "entertaining" at a beautiful Thai restaurant in Oxford. It must have been about October as it was pretty chilly and the evening was going beautifully until it came to the bill.

Boldly whipping my company card out, I said, "I'll

pick this up".

I tapped in my pin number.

AUTH DEC

Otherwise known as Authorisation Declined.

The waitress said, "I'll try it again as sometimes it plays up."

She did

Dialing…

I tapped in my pin number. Again.

AUTH DEC

I could feel my face burning up, the other diners began to benefit by warming their hands on my red cheeks.

"Try it again please."

Still same result.

I was kinda like the Auth Dec equivalent of a reverse Michael Owen, a hat-trick of own goals.

The client I was with said, "Not a problem" and went over to the cash machine and got the cash out which I would pay them back the next day.

How embarrassing… It was all set to get worse, as I then had to pay the Oxford hotel I was staying at in the morning… they'd done the old £1 pre-auth thing…

I wakes up at the crack of dawn, sauntering past the lady on reception, giving her my best "I'll be back this evening, I've got lots of important business meetings on, I'm a very important business man you know… with lots of money in the bank" kinda nod and head hurriedly out the door.

Later that morning while driving, I get a call from the hotel to say the card has been declined.

I mumble something about a changeover protocol, which meant as much to me as it did to the lady who called.

I said I'd get my PA to give her a call and sort out an alternative payment immediately. The "PA" in this case was my wife with her personal credit card. As you can appreciate she was delighted. It was like one of those cartoons where you hear an angry/squeaky/rapid voice on the other side of the phone kicking off.

Sailing close to the wind seems to be a by-product of going it alone.

I spoke to Stef Thomas of *www.noredbraces.co.uk* and he had an equally amusing/cringeworthy story to share.

66 I had an appointment to meet a contact in north London. Someone I had done some work for who wanted to meet up and see what else I could do for them. Really worthwhile opportunity for me with someone I already had some rapport with. We spoke most days on the phone and I knew that he liked to do 'the deal' face-to-face.

I had been in business for a year or so I guess and it was one of those months when everyone was late paying. The night before I was due to go and see him I tried to fill the car with petrol but my card was declined. Simple truth was I had no cash until someone else paid me. I had enough petrol to get to the meeting but probably not enough to drive home again.

So what to do? Phone the guy and explain to him? Make up some excuse? I went and had the meeting. Won the business. He's still a client now.

That small decision proved to me that I had the tenacity for this thing. I lived my life and my business like that for a couple of years, always stretching the most out of each and every last pound. Making sure that the wheels just stayed on and that the business kept going. I didn't think it was that clever at the time, but looking back, it is quite possibly the one thing that separated me from other businesses that aren't here anymore.

I kept going. I pushed through when I had less than no money. And I took risks when others decided to give up and get a 'safe' job.

Did I get home? Just…

Those last 30 miles with the 'empty' light on and no plan B aren't great for the nerves, but I made it. **"**

You're going to have days like that when it feels like swimming The Channel: you get halfway across when a painful stitch kicks in. You feel like giving up, but hang about! It's as far back as it is forward, so keep pressing on.

Moments like the above are sent to test whether you have the *testicular fortitude* to cut it in business. Because if you survive against all odds, the challenges you will face later are a doddle. It sets you up for your future business success.

The first half of the journey is the tough bit.

It's no lie when in GOYA I talked about delivering pizza,

living on Tesco *Value* fish fingers and beans every night, funded through a jar of 2ps and 1ps. All my life I'd been skint, so I was no stranger to AUTH DEC on my personal accounts. The same couldn't be said for Terry Cooper (TC), Development Director of 4Networking. This is a guy who had 30 years on a main board PLC, a proud man, who I'd bet on my life had never been overdrawn in his life.

Our Terry does everything by the letter and he's not one for cutting corners with profit and loss sheets. When it comes to buying a round of drinks he's as tight as a duck's arse, although he is getting better!

Back then 4N had just 3 Directors and TC and I were bombing around the UK to 4N meets. 1000 miles each week was the norm.

On this particular day, he rang in to say that he was in the garage and had had a knockback on his card: the current account was empty.

"I'm sorry TC. Look – we're on it and gonna sort it out."

"I know Brad, it's just frustrating."

"Again, I'm sorry fella… really."

Terry believed in 4Networking, paid for the fuel out of his own pocket and continued his journey.

We ALL had to hold our nerve, hold our line, hold onto our belief even when faced with overwhelming evidence to the contrary.

Then the unthinkable happened. For the second time in three days, Terry rang in again to say insufficient funds. Tim Johnson and I just looked at each other.

This was a company on the edge, the edge of failure, teetering on bankruptcy.

Why was that? In *GOYA* I alluded to this situation, but never fleshed it out.

So here's what happened. We're at an Area Leader's meeting in Birmingham, about 30 or so 4N Area and Regional Leaders in attendance and Mr Hot-Head here suggests that we don't need to actively sell memberships any more as 4Networking is such a great network that people will join anyway.

Or so I thought. Even 'marketing geniuses' get it wrong. Sometimes.

As a result, weekly revenues dropped by 75%... SEVENTY FIVE PERCENT.

If my memory serves me correctly, our then £10k per week revenue dropped to just under £3k.

SHIT.

When you're running a tight ship anyway, losing ¾ of your revenue is a big deal. Even more so when you have £0 reserves.

I was sending cheques without signatures, only to have them returned with a letter asking for a signature. I'd become more like a market trader than a Managing Director through those dark months.

Hairy and scary times.

We had a combination of not having our web solution fully in place in order to make easy membership sign-up happen, and me making a decision on the assumption that it would work soon... which it hasn't fully to this day... we're on it though.

Now even if we had had the automated web solution which signposted to members what to do and how to join, it probably wouldn't have achieved the sign-up rate we needed because people just don't respond in a simple way to online sign-up requests.

The world of processes and structures is great and works 100% of the time for flow charts and computer programmers, but when dealing with people there are so many variables which automated business models can never take into account.

Remember – worry about processes when you've stopped worrying about sales!

In the face-to-face world, people sometimes do need to be invited to join, to be encouraged, to have the benefits spelt out to them. This doesn't mean turning into an uber sales person, handling objections and all that guff, it just means creating an easy "invitation to join."

Or perhaps in your case, "Would you like to go ahead with a trial of X service or product?"

Products rarely sell themselves unless you're flogging *iPads*. I've said previously that you need to create the conditions where people buy, and this stands. However, you still need to do as much of the sell as possible before you 'sell'. Effectively, you've got to make it as easy as possible for people to buy. A sale is done in the first two minutes, not the last, and people buy from people before they buy products and services.

I talked before about the world of employment being like this:

Payday – SKINT – Payday – SKINT – Payday – SKINT – Payday – SKINT – Payday – SKINT – Payday – SKINT

Starting a business off goes like this:

SKINT – SKINT – SKINT – SKINT – Half Payday – SKINT – SKINT – SKINT – SKINT – Half Payday – SKINT – SKINT – SKINT – SKINT – Payday – Payday – Payday – Payday

This is how it's gone on for us for SIX years.

The reason you are skint in those start-up years is because either you or your business gets fed, not both!

Back in 1981, my dad could often be found in the bookies studying form and the racing papers, betting what little money he had. One day he placed a Yankee bet at the bookies: you bet on 7 horses, if you horse wins, the bet goes forward to the next and you either win big or lose it all.

He won big: £15,000. We had nothing in 1981, so this was massive. Although, like everything back then, it was easy come, easy go.

My dad did take me on an amazingly memorable holiday to California for three weeks – this was the biggest holiday of my life. Previous holidays had never been anything more exotic than Sunny Vale Caravan Park in Rhyl, North Wales for a week.

My father wasn't a rich man, yet he always had massive aspirations to be a millionaire and would often do whatever he deemed OK in order to make money.

I'm not the kind of bloke you'll see at the bookies – I have to ask someone to help me fill in the Grand National betting slip. However, I do wonder if some of that gambling win big/lose big mindset has been passed my way. Up until recently I've always had 5 metaphorical horses in on my business Yankee.

So for the first and only time in my life, I went on a big holiday with my dad and he told me that like him, I too would take my children to Disney World when they were seven years old.

I used to wonder how I would manage to make this happen…

And this year I did, finally being in a position to afford to go on a holiday to Disney in Florida, taking my THREE lads with me. The words of my dad from 30 years ago acted as a goal, which I've finally fulfilled.

This reminds me of a story that Martin Byrne (*martin@businessprotect.biz*) shared with me about his boy Phoenix, who at the time was 9. Our Martin is so rock and roll he can play drums *and* guitar *and* he called his son Phoenix! When he's not providing key man insurance etc for businesses, lives the rock and roll lifestyle. He used to be in a band but when his kids came along he had to give this up.

He still keeps his hand in and he started teaching Phoenix

how to play guitar. Using a classic Jimi Hendrix track as backing, Phoenix kept trying but gave up, crying, "I can't play it". Martin turned to his lad and said, "Getting it wrong is all part of getting it right – in order to get it right you have to get it wrong first. No one picks up a guitar and plays a song perfectly first time. At some point in his life, Jimi Hendrix couldn't play guitar – he had to pick it up and learn it."

With that, Martin wiped away his boy's tears and within an hour, both father and son played it faultlessly, every bit as good as Hendrix!

So remember, no one is born an expert.

No one. "An expert is a person who has made all the mistakes that can be made in a very narrow field." Niels Bohr, Danish physicist (1885-1962)

I love that!

OK, back to my dad and carrying on his Disney legacy...

On the surface our trip to Disney World Florida was just a holiday, but I decided to also make use of it as an opportunity to seek out examples of how the best businesses in the Sunshine State remain at the top of their game.

Here's what I found.

At Disney World we had a blast, but I practically had to re-mortgage my house to buy the tickets.

The parks cost a fortune to run and maintain but, boy, do they engage their audience. How? They constantly reinvest. From a conversation I had with a cast member, they have upwards of 60,000 trained, seemingly enthused, upbeat employees working the parks every day. That's a serious wage bill, but you get what you pay for. At Disney World not only do you get a safe, clean, exciting kids utopia, you also get to see a utopia of how great business can be when it's constantly revised, tweaked and financed. This is what happens when you slingshot from IN- to Sufficient funds.

You know what I loved most about Disney World? Every ten minutes the dollars seemed to flow out of my pocket. Sodas, Mickey Mouse merchandise, ride photos, they all cost extra. And yet it didn't matter because we were having so much fun, so much holiday.

Along with everyone else, I got caught up in the whole Disney dollars decadence. There were mornings when it felt less like a holiday and more like I was planning an amphibious commando raid – up at the crack of dawn, with a breakfast table full of theme park maps to work out the best route to hit the big rides fast.

Disney is a business with a culture of constant reinvestment.

The more money comes in, the more money gets reinvested.

It's the same with 4Networking – it's a winning strategy for business.

You walk around and they empty your pockets with a big Disney smile on their face. It's an amazing experience, an amazing business. Worth every cent.

The lessons for your business from this are to engage, to make people feel good but in a genuine way, because when people feel good, they are more likely to buy.

There is a war going on in Florida, with all the big theme parks engaged in it. Sea World, Islands of Adventure, Busch Gardens and Universal are all competing for those tourist bucks. This is great for the consumer because those parks that don't invest in new rides, attractions and facilities are the ones that won't be around in 5 years time.

In Kissimmee in Florida is an 'old school' fun park with no entrance fee: you just pay for what you go on. It can't compete with the big budgets of the major parks so it doesn't even try.

But what it does offer is one particular ride as dramatic as any of those found in the big parks – the world's tallest Skycoaster, *www.skycoaster.cc*. Think 300 foot rugby posts, you get into a safety harness with a massive bungie type cord on it and a mechanical winch takes you up to the top face down.

Big Ben is 316 foot.

You hear instructions from a speaker: 3, 2, 1, pull the ripcord...

Absolutely terrifying. You pull the release... and then it becomes really terrifying. You plummet head first towards the ground before the bungee cord is fully extended at which point you begin flying like Superman, turning fear into elation and excitement.

I did it...

If you ever go to Florida please give it a go. It's an amazingly effective thrill ride, yet in terms of sophistication and cost, it's pretty basic and will have been relatively cheap to set up. Compare the Skycoaster website with that of the big parks: just like the ride, it's very basic, but they've somehow carved out a memorable superlative amongst all the other Florida attractions – it IS The World's Tallest Skycoaster. The business lessons are clear - to compete with larger competitors, do it on your terms, not theirs.

And as scary as things get, there are times when you have to take the brave decision to pull your ripcord otherwise you will be stuck going nowhere.

Enough theme park stories for now.

Actually, 4Networking Florida would be ace.

Outrageous goal?

Maybe once, but not anymore, it will happen!

Also while in Florida, on the recommendation of a friend, I had "Visit Hooters" on my TO DO list. You may have heard of it. It's a 'restaurant' where the waitresses wear orange hot pants and skinny vests –

Bold

it looks like something straight out of a seventies porn film.

Before I set off, my friend explained that Hooters had reinvented itself. No longer a macho, beer-swilling, football-watching place for drunken blokes to go and ogle the waitresses, it had become, believe it or not, a family-friendly venue.

So with that I persuaded the wife that we'd give it a look and mosey on down with my boys. Take it from me. Hooters has NOT reinvented itself... ha, nice joke...

Not that I'm complaining.

Predictably, I loved it. As did every other bloke in there. It was absolutely rammed with guys wearing American Football tops shouting "DEFENCE!" at at one of the tens of plasma screens showing sports around the venue.

I was so impressed with the whole thing, analysing carefully the 'business element', of course. There was the branding, the Hooters girls (who should all be nominated for Oscars, as every guy felt at ease following the deft way they laughed at all the rubbish jokes and pretended to be interested in every single one of us), the approach, the boobies, the wings.

It was like a surreal theme park where overweight, balding blokes (and there were a lot of us) could watch sports, be fed by hot women and could feel special. You know you are being hustled but you don't care.

Chicken wings were served by waitresses with big perfect-teeth smiles, with an extra nudge and a wink and the dollars just eased themselves out of our pocket with upsells. Of course I left a tip, the biggest one of the holiday! The wife, she also enjoyed the experience, buying herself a Hooters t-shirt. Now I'm UK-side, wifey's re-creation of the experience will probably only go as far as the occasional wearing of the t-shirt and still no laughing at my jokes.

Chicken wings, boobs and Mickey Mouse ears aside, should you find yourself in the US, both Hooters and Disney World are essential visits. You will understand what makes them so special and how mixing business with pleasure works. Just tell your wife that Brad Burton says that Hooters has "reinvented itself as a family venue".

And in answer to my question, what have Disney World and Hooters got in common? I'll tell you: great customer service, giving the customer, their target market, what they want. The lesson?

Create desire and stuff sells itself.

Disney World and Hooters use the same business model.

They both mix business and pleasure, because it works.

Both these businesses have massive reinvestment, a constant ploughing of money back into the whole business machine to keep their business fresh, relevant and adapting to the changing needs of their customers.

Get the basics of your business right before getting too clever. But once you've cracked that, always strive for CONSTANT improvement. How many people start making money and then sit back and stop developing?

The key is to refine and perfect, constantly.

Back to my business. The reality has now caught up with the vision: in fact it's surpassed it! So another outrageous goal is now needed.

The World's Largest Joined-up Business Network... It'll happen.

People have stopped laughing now.

In fact, initially, starting and sustaining just 5 networking groups was a tough job. Although this has since grown to 300+ linked groups and become a multi-million pound business, 4N nearly didn't get past those first 5. The point I'm making is that even with hard graft and great ideas the line between success and failure is a narrow one.

Also, although it helps if you start out with a great vision, with us, to be truthful, the first 4N group was set up just as a way to get me appointments for my existing marketing business!

Danny Slevin, *www.objective-eye.co.uk*, told me about his first year of business:

❝ I found it quite refreshing to find out how little money you can actually live on. It's a bit like stripping your life down to the bare bones and starting again from scratch.

It's only then you realise how you overspent when you were an employee. Still miss certain luxuries, like meat. Start your own business and basically become a vegetarian. They didn't cover that on the Business Link 'Preparing for self-employment' course. ❞

Insufficient funds are OK on your road to success.
Insufficient desire is not.

Sometimes you have to risk everything, to make it right.

CHAPTER 10
There is no cavalry

So I tips up at the job centre, unmotivated, unshaven, truth be known I couldn't even afford razors, apart from those cheap single blade disposable ones which were *big time* painful to use and guaranteed to cause cuts. It was as bad a morning as any other back then. The bloke looked over his half-moon glasses and snootily asked, "And what have you done to look for work?"

The truth was, I had done nothing – at that time it was a big enough struggle to get out of bed for 10am once a fortnight to sign on. However, I covered my lies with a few hastily ripped out adverts from Thursday's *Bristol Evening Post* job section, which allowed Mr Snooty to tick his KPI box.

What's different about the Brad above and the one who is writing this book is the last 10 years' journey.

It's not that I was lazy – I just lost my way.

At various points in our lives, we all lose our way, allowing the lazy to kick in. Sometimes it's getting blindsided by something that causes us to not want to move forward, so we are then frozen by inaction, waiting like a life raft at sea for something or someone to come along to rescue us and reverse our fortunes.

It just doesn't work like that. It's totally down to you.

The government right now, the Con-Libs, are committed to slashing the welfare budget. They want to get the unemployed back to work, they want to remove that BIIIIG slice of welfare out of the Treasury's coffers and assign that money to a more worthy cause, MP's expenses perhaps?

Having been long-term unemployed, that's about 4 years in total of signing on, my view is that in order to get "people like me" back into work and into the system, you need to get to them fast to ensure that the rot doesn't take hold.

Having also been long-term *self-unemployed*, the same rules apply.

You need something to believe in.

Give people a genuine belief that things can be better because without it, it's nigh on impossible to get your shots off.

In my time I've had a few bosses who have told me they

were "determined to make me a millionaire."

Each time I've heard that, I've thought, "I've made it". In fact the line was being wheeled out as a Dilbert management wheeze to get me to work harder or to not leave the company.

But amazingly, each time I heard it, I did genuinely feel that anything was possible, that I could become a millionaire just by believing and hanging onto the coat-tails of those that had already made it.

The truth, however...

...it rarely works like that. It's down to you. I've already said that there are no *Millionaire Makers* as such. But you can watch and learn from successful people, which is what I've made a habit of doing. Switch on your *Reticular Activation* and see properly what you are looking for – sounds like something you'd see in a *Terminator* movie. Whenever you meet someone in a business capacity, ask yourself what is it they are doing that you really like and equally what can you observe them doing that sucks.

It's habit-forming and before you know it you begin to change subtly. You always have your base and your foundations of who you are. But you will begin to pick up improved new traits and skills and discard the elements that you discover not to be working.

Study everyone – copy no one.

If you've never heard of Reticular Activation, give it a Google, it really works.

"One man bands don't work", Tim Johnson cheerfully shared with a room full of 4Networkers and he's right, albeit delivered in his unique, if slightly autistic, approach to motivating people. However, the problem in being a one man band is you have to do everything yourself. It's down to you: you have limited resources, so you have to make every minute of real work count.

The answer is to find others that can fill in those skill gaps and can be the cement in the foundations of your business. Big business has departments and so can you. Sub-contractors who act as all the departments you need: marketing, accounts, systems, administration, HR. Although our business is now of significant size, we still use sub-contractors all day long – here's a selection of some of ours.

My PA, Jacqui Turner (*jacqui@thetweetingpa.co.uk*)

Creative director (*www.extrabold.biz*)

Media production team (*www.mediapartnership.co.uk*)

PR team (*www.avidpr.co.uk*)

Editor (*www.lexiconmarketing.co.uk*)

Use subbies and build your business, whilst building theirs. It really is a win-win situation. Create yourself that virtual company you've always dreamed of.

After all, "There are not enough hours in the day". If you've ever said this or heard someone say it, keep a diary and jot down a word or line every 15 minutes which describes what you've done.

I promise you that between 1h 45m and 3 days from when you initiate this practice you'll realise that there are enough hours in the day. If you find there aren't, it's just you're dicking about.

Yup. I've tried this with loads of people who tell me there are not enough hours in the day. It's bullshit.

Make the hours work, stop talking yourself out of things and start talking yourself into things.

Find the time, as your success or failure is now down to you.

Gary Gorman, *www.garygorman.co.uk*, is back:

66 The thing about corporate life is that you can always blame someone else.

'It's marketing's fault, they're on credit hold, we've got no stock, the competitors grabbed the best site, the buyer won't see me'. However... in the real world... there are no excuses, no alibis, no one to blame. The Lone Ranger and Tonto are not around the corner.

If you don't do it... it ain't gonna happen. 99

So true Gary, so true.

Don't go running around chasing new biz until you've been paid for existing work. Take control of your credit – impose seven day accounts, ask for 50% deposits, don't be embarrassed to ring up and ask where your payment is, instead of, "Hi X, sorry to bother you, I'm just chasing up invoice number #423, as it's 3 weeks overdue".

Get hard-core, in a nice way, but get hard-core: without money in your bank the pressure builds and that spills into other areas of your life. If you've done the job, you should get paid.

Dee Uzoka (*http://va-in-medway.co.uk/*) said,

66 I lost my balance, that fragile alliance with your own head. Enthusiasm is indeed that and a personal issue which can then permeate all the way through into your work, and the next thing, you lose your balance – it's like a wobbly box cart wheel. 99

It's only a matter of time before the wheels come off. So, take no prisoners, work with people who don't take the piss but who value you and your services.

And at those times when you're thinking, "This is all too tough", it's still better than working for someone else for 40 hours plus 18hrs travelling time each week. Surely?

Just accept that the road of a one wom/man band is a tough one, so get yourself a support team, people who you can be truly honest with about how you are feeling. These friends will have no vested interest other than a willingness to see you succeed, because they care for you.

Sleeping during the day is something which I actively encourage people who run a business from home to do.

What I mean is, work when you are upbeat and chipper and if you are slumping and not together, don't feel guilty about having a catnap. I'm always at it. When you step into the ring, you are going to need to be in tip-top condition. Get a call answering service and you'll never miss an enquiry while catnapping.

Initially, while building a business or a new venture, you'll find yourself doing things for free. In my case it has been speaking gigs to develop my profile. That's OK, it really is, as it's a great way to build up experience, create a client base, win testimonials and develop a lead base. There does then come a point when you have to change to "I'll spend my time when you spend your money" mode.

Along the way you'll be tempted by people who claim that you can buy your business success with marketing, PR and advertising. Over the last 5 years I've spent tens of thousands on that lot and it's all fabulous, *as long as you can afford for it not to work!*

The lesson in all this is that in the lean times, it's not expensive marketing campaigns which are gonna dig you out of the shit, it's sales. And all you need for that is shoe leather and a phone, plus it helps if you've got a decent product!

But if money is tight, every activity you undertake for your business should be designed to get you in front of someone, to gain an appointment.

Here's something you can do right now to move you closer to getting in front of people which is damn effective and as near to free as possible.

Grab your mobile and start going through your 'loose' contact list,

start at A and then just DIAL or DELETE.

"But what should I say?" I hear you ask.

Just speak, try this.

"Hi X, just thought I'd give you a bell to catch up and see how you are getting on…"

And let it free flow… then if after the call it's a relationship that you feel is going nowhere and there is no real connection, delete the number.

It's really powerful because it does two things: it gets you in a mind-set that moves you and your relationships on and it closes down the ones that are going nowhere, freeing you up to concentrate on those that may go somewhere.

It's better to have 10 decent contacts than 100 phone numbers.

Personal emails, letters and calls, leveraging personal contacts, all of this is free or as free as it can be. So do it… today. Don't put it off by protesting that you don't like doing it: if you are working for yourself, sorry to break it to you, but this is what you signed up for.

Don't be over eager to rush your personal development.

Experience takes time and you are never going to be an expert in your field when you start. Accept that you are going to get more "No's" than "Yes's" along the way.

But also be aware that picking the wrong fight at an early stage could result in a knockdown you don't get up from. KO at this stage of the game could ruin you.

I recall just before I shut down my first biz, 4Consultancy, to go full time onto 4Networking, I landed a £16k print job. I was high fiving like crazy…

Then the reality sank in, that actually this £16k job was in fact just £1500 profit and a shit load of work and risk. Had the job gone wrong, I would have been in no position to sort it, ie fund getting it reprinted, and that would have been the end of my business.

So, be careful what you chase down in business, because the headline figure can turn out to be a BIG risk. If I asked you to place a £14,500 bet in order to win £1500 you'd say, not a chance, yet that's what it was, a gamble.

One time I got a phone call from a company asking if I did language translations. I said, "Sure. What languages?" They said, "French, Spanish and Portuguese". I said "Send me the text over and I'll get you a price".

The text came through and I sent back an email quoting £375: they accepted.

I then went on Google, found the translation website BabelFish, *www.babelfish.com* and used it to translate the work.

The client was delighted with the result, so much so that I ended up getting two further jobs from them. Absolute true story.

More often than not, in those early days, you have to be inventive: say "No" to nothing and worry about it out after, but just don't bite off more than you can sensibly chew, as per that big print job.

So, these appointments you need. Think about the people you know, who do they know and how can they actively get you in front of your target audience?

Dial or Delete?

It's all about inspiration.

Inspiration creates action, action creates results.

In *GOYA* I talked about a song I listen to whenever I feel low, *The Only Way Is Up* by Yazz & The Plastic Population. I've got another couple for you: fire up YouTube and find *Breakout* by Swingout Sister and whilst you're at it, *Ain't No Stopping Us Now* by McFadden & Whitehead, plus a little wildcard for you, this has massive poignancy for me, *Anything* by Jay Z.

Listen to them each a couple of times, they are absolute belters at helping you get your *Scalextric* cars back on track and you back into the groove. I don't think I'm alone in these weird rituals.

I'd also recommend you give *www.Smarta.com* a look. It's a massive free video resource, including loads of interviews with entrepreneurs. It's well worth a cup of tea and half an hour of your time, if you find yourself dicking about.

Life is a seesaw of resource: family, friends, work, personal, gym, telly, travelling. Often, something has to give and we made the decision as a family that I would have to sacrifice everything else for the first few years while we got into orbit.

I was told more times than I can remember that I had no chance with 4Networking and had I listened to the buzz killers they would have been right!

I also got bored of listening to my negative internal voice, the doubting self, and said, "Bollocks, this is *your* time to make it happen, Brad. You can. No you *WILL* do this". I'd tell myself this when I had quiet time.

Those internal battles with yourself, take them on today.

Right now, as in right now.

Have it out NOW, I'll hold your coat.

As you transition from employment into self-employment you'll find yourself looking back to the past for answers. But it's a different world now and the past isn't going to help you.

It's down to you. Time & a halving is out, as are paid holidays. Forget it.

I recall that awful realisation, when as a 16 year-old in my first job, I was given the news that there was no six week summer holiday.

One 4N member I know who had a creative business was being approached for web work all day long and kept turning it away. I suggested that they set up their own web development arm and use sub-contractors to fulfil the work. All of a sudden by saying "Yes" they worked it out, and pulled the work in. Just perfect: use other members to help you AND them get ahead, everyone wins!

One day I was driving to London with Tim Johnson in my then new car and I wanted to switch on the automatic traffic announcements. I randomly poked and prodded the many buttons on the car stereo, hoping to get lucky and switch it on. Tim watched me do this and then calmly worked out where the appropriate TA (Traffic Announcement ON) button was before engaging his finger and switching it straight on.

That's the difference: I'm all suck it and see, Tim's more read the list of ingredients and only then consider sucking it! Ooh matron, *Carry On GOYA*.

No one can afford to keep doing things twice. So don't.

Assemble yourself a team that helps you to get it right first time as often as possible.

Running a business isn't about looking at spreadsheets day in, day out, but it is about getting stuck in and doing whatever is necessary to first stay alive and then get ahead.

Once you realise that there is no cavalry unless you recruit it, the future is yours to shape.

I got knocked down over and over again, but I got back up on my feet and kept on fighting, as did Sharon Wright, *http://motherofinventionbook.co.uk/*, check her out on Google. She's the woman who went on *Dragons' Den* and arguably gave the best pitch in the history of the show. All the Dragons fought to invest in both her and her product *Magnamole*.

Her elation was followed by an acrimonious fallout with one of the Dragons, resulting in a heavy fight which completely derailed both her and her business: Google it to read all about it.

I know her personally and even though I thought she was mad taking on such a fight, she truly believed that she had been wronged.

When you are right in the eye of a business shit-storm, like we were when 4Networking began and we took the then market leader head on, no one looking in from outside can fathom why you are taking on these almighty battles for what seems like little gain.

But like Sharon, even when faced with overwhelming odds, there was no plan B.

You too can find the strength needed to keep going if you truly believe in what you are fighting for.

All that glitters isn't always gold. Sometimes you don't need anyone else, sometimes you do, but only you can make that decision.

Sometimes the only cavalry/support you can rely on, as in really rely on, is yourself, unless of course like me you're lucky enough to have a *truly supportive wife/partner.*

There is no cavalry, unless you create it

CHAPTER 11
Look Mum, I'm on telly – Car Keyers

So we've gone from getting a small piece in the *Highbridge & Burnham-on-Sea Gazette* to getting national media coverage – I've even appeared on the now defunct BBC2 business show, *Working Lunch*. In case you're wondering, the decision to bin the 10 year-old programme was made 2 days before my appearance... but it does make you wonder!

I also now find myself being a regular contributor on Jeremy Vine's Radio 2 show. After my first appearance, it became clear I wasn't afraid to speak my mind, especially to 'Disgusted of Tunbridge Wells' type callers to his phone-in segment. I just seem to delight in coming up with an original angle, in finding ways of undermining the accepted wisdom on a particular topic. You know what I think about accepted wisdom: it's normally dull, old school thinking which needs binning...

Anyway, a piece of national media coverage which has made me write this chapter is the two page spread which appeared in *The Independent*'s 'Wealth Check' feature: you can see it here: *http://ind.pn/bradburton*

Since its publication, I've heard of a number of people who have decided to use this piece to take a pop at me. The red rag to the bull appears to be the phrase, "He currently earns about £100,000 a year".

This seems to have kicked up a shit-storm of resentment based around this sort of argument: "How dare someone who is running a business have the audacity to be making some money himself?" In fact, up until (very) recently, I've always been skint and now finally, for the first time in 37 years I am finally touching some success. Instead of *touching cloth* each time I went to fill up the car.

Is that really such a crime?

Over the course of the last 6 years of self-employment, it's only in the last 12 months or so that things have really begun to work out for us as an organisation. That's 6 looooong years of under-investment in terms of family life and personal money to get this network up and running.

So why on earth should self-employed people resent hard work and sacrifice finally paying off? Isn't that what the vision of successful self-employment should be all about?

I'm not alone on this by the way, but I seem to have been particularly singled out because I'm now in the public eye.

Is 6 years of struggle not enough for you?

I'm hardly crying myself to sleep: on the contrary, it drives me. I previously used doubters and now negative energy to keep me hungry and sharp. As hungry as I was on my first day of self-employment.

Not long ago, I too was a doubter who had the effect of driving someone else to achieve something which seemed impossible. Let me explain.

4Networking's National Development Leader, Gary Johannes, told me he was setting out on what he called **BRAVE** – Bike Ride Across Vietnam Event. *BRAVE?* More like stupid and I told him so! The idea was for Gary and his son Christopher to ride 650km across a mountainous part of Vietnam for a charity whose work had deeply affected him and his family – The National Spinal Injuries Children's Ward at Stoke Mandeville. Gary's motivation for doing this was highly personal, as a few years ago, following an accident, the Spinal Injuries Children's Ward, seemingly miraculously, brought his son Christopher back from chest-down paralysis to being able to walk and... cycle.

Anyway, Gary's nearly as fat as me, so I reckoned he had no chance and I told him as much. I even bet him £250 that he couldn't do it and offered a £100 donation to the Stoke Mandeville charity before he set off if he admitted as much. You can read more and see the full story of the outcome here: *http://bit.ly/GaryBlog*.

If you haven't got access to read about it on the 'net, what happened is that YES, BIG Gary J completed the bike ride, all 650km of it, raised some valuable dosh for the charity, had an amazing shared experience with his son, and basically produced a performance that was so unexpected that there had to be an extra dimension to his motivation.

My doubting him was part of that, as he said – "Brad, you should never have placed that bet, as I hate to fail, and your doubting gave me extra strength when in agony climbing those tough mountains, as did all the great support from my friends and

Gary and his son Christopher at the summit of the final hill

family. Good on you for paying your debt!" So, when someone laughs in your face, whether it's me or someone else saying, "It'll never work", use that as kindling to get your motivation up. As Gary has showed, you really can achieve things which look way out of reach.

So, well done Slim, what a result! £250 of my smackers ended up going to the Stoke Mandeville charity, which is still welcoming donations here: *www.justgiving.com/BRAVE-UK*.

So, if you find people bitching and sniping as a result of your successes, don't get dragged down by them – keep your focus, life and energy on continually creating positive momentum rather than getting wrapped up in the neg heads' world.

I've made my sacrifices and so will you on that road to 'making it'.

Chris Hatch, *www.zedoarydesign.co.uk*, shared with me his view:

❝ The people who run down your achievements, aspirations and dreams do so because they either have none of their own or they are too scared to take the risk because their fear of being seen to fail exceeds their dreams. It's always important to remember that they don't matter and what they talk about today will be tomorrow's chip paper. Ultimately there is only one person that needs to believe in your dream, only one person that can gauge your success. **❞**

Listen, I'm under no illusions that our success is down to a team effort. Although I front it up and I am often the one in the spotlight, without the personal sacrifices, hard graft and belief of the other directors, all the teams, our members and our suppliers, the company couldn't and wouldn't exist.

I thank my lucky stars every single day for the 'luck' and the series of decisions and people that have helped us to become the powerhouse across the UK, soon to be the globe.

The network was born so that I didn't have to deliver pizzas. The business world for SMEs is tough, damn tough, and I always tell it like it is, but if we as small businesses huddle together we've all got a much better chance of succeeding.

At some point in your life you will also come across people who have it in for you.

You could be the Dalai Lama and someone would still want to take a pot shot at you for your stance on world peace.

Tamsen Garrie (4N Network Director) told me she'd had similar feedback about me and although she wouldn't give me any names, she quite rightly passed this on to me, in the nice Tamsen way that she does things.

> ❝ I think it's a good thing, as it shows that our success strategy is working. Our strategy for success is based around one thing: Member Success. EVERYTHING we do is with this in mind – that's why we've managed to develop at such an exceptional rate, because our intentions are correct.
>
> 4Networking is a national business and personal development platform which enables success for its members.
>
> Part of enabling success is leading it and part of leading is demonstrating it. That means creating it for ourselves.
>
> What value is there in having an MD who is skint?
>
> Is that what members want as an example of how 4N can enable success? I know which I'd prefer to aspire to. ❞

She's so right. A way to demonstrate the success of the network has been to make it work for us and for our teams and that's what we've done.

At the beginning of any plane journey you'll hear a safety briefing, "In the event of an emergency, place your own oxygen mask on, before helping others."

BANG ON.

You as in YOU can't help anyone until you ensure that you've got your own shit together.

Part of our whole media push right now is a direct result of my seminars. I'm flat out every week, up and down the country, speaking at conferences, schools, networking events. I can do this not as a result of some intense training, but purely from practising week in, week out at breakfast meetings, just like any other member of 4N can, 4 days a week.

Sorry to keep going on about 4N, but it's right at the centre of my success, and if you're the kind of person that 'gets it', it'll be right at the core of yours too.

It can be the rocket fuel you need for your business, friendship and personal development.

Get speaking as often as you can. This is how it panned out for me (because I made it happen). Each one of these speaking gigs will give you an opportunity to develop your style, refine your delivery and recognise the small nuances which you will learn to use to lift a presentation into a great performance.

Back to my speaking – in general my speaking gigs are to adults and business people, but I had the opportunity to speak to a group of 11 young teens from disadvantaged backgrounds in Swindon and I shared with them my story of why I moved from Manchester (chapter 2). These kids got it straightaway and understood the situation, which shows that up and down the country there are other children living equally shitty lives.

Maybe that's something I'll end up doing down the line: talking to kids that I'm proof positive that good can come from adversity, even though at the time the shit is happening, it makes no sense.

Do check out *www.innerflame.org.uk*, perhaps you too can help them to continue to make a positive difference.

In the early days of speaking, I had loads of energy and pizzazz but no one could understand me.

The truth is, I spoke too fast. I knew what I wanted to put across but somehow the audience often didn't 'get it'.

You will get it wrong more times than you get it right in those early days, but you can't speed up experience that you may lack.

Using your gob in business is the most powerful tool in the world and better still, it's FREE.

At that time, I was close to blagging my way onto bigger stages, but that would have been a big mistake. So, like a band just starting out, I paid my dues, touring the country, playing small venues until my set was good enough to do some (almost) stadium gigs.

Start small and build up your confidence and experience before going for bigger targets. Resist the temptation to go big too fast.

Now, whenever I do a TV appearance or radio interview, twitter is awash with people playing Brad Bingo, seeing what Brad phrases will crop up. Recently, someone even tweeted a photo of a whiteboard in their office:

Pizza ✓

Private number plates ✓

Spinny chairs ✓

At some of the speaking gigs I do now, I get proper 5 star treatment. I'm tempted to come over all Jennifer Lopez, demanding Egyptian cotton sheets on my dressing room walls, ionisers and crystal bowls of blue Smarties. In fact I'm still enjoying the novelty of being put up in hotels that are so posh that I have trouble closing my suitcase, the towels are so thick…

When re-watching myself on the BBC2 *Working Lunch* programme my wife said to me, "I don't know how they managed to make you look so fat. They say that being on telly puts on an extra 10 pounds; in the era of HD it seems to have put on 10 kilos."

BRAD
BINGO

- They said it would never work
- Aggressively waiting for the phone to ring
- Not as thick as I look
- 'Supportive' wife
- Cufflinking
- Living the dream
- Fish tanks, personal numberplates and spinny chairs
- Calm yourselves ladies

I'm fat, but I'm not that fat. Am I? Judge for yourself here: *http://bit.ly/BradWorkingLunch*. Going on national live TV was as exciting as it was scary. I was busting for a squizz, but since the show goes out live I had to sit it out until the show was over… The point here is that 4 years prior to this I was

sat in my box room in my underpants aggressively waiting for the phone to ring before going downstairs to watch *Working Lunch/Jeremy Kyle" (*Delete as applicable).

Let me share with you The Mysterious Case of Dave Sands. It sounds like a frigging Sherlock Holmes story, but this is no work of fiction.

I was booked to speak at an event somewhere in the East Midlands and when I arrived I was taken gently to one side by the organiser and told about "anonymous warnings" that had been received about me.

So there I am with Young Enterprise East Midlands, to talk to a group of early teen kids about entrepreneurism and the organisers are getting a little nervous at the thought of that somehow. If the contents of Dave Sands' emails were to be believed, they had mistakenly booked the Chubby Brown of the business world. Who could blame them, after seeing the cobblers that had landed in their inbox?

The same went for the Federation of Small Business event in Kettering. With my ear to the ground of a national business network, it didn't take long for the information to filter back as to who Dave Sands really was: a pseudonym for someone filled with anger and jealousy towards me as it happens.

And then up pops 'Wendy B', posting a comment on a

blog I'm mentioned in on the Telegraph website. Here are some choice excerpts:

❝ You've swanned around telling a lot of people half truths, exaggerations and a right load of hyperbolic old nonsense about your background.

You grew up on "the mean streets of Salford". Would it harm you to say you had an unremarkable and relatively comfortable upbringing free from gangsters and illegal activities?

Your contradictions are hilarious, your pronouncements about "biz" are old hat and I'm afraid 3k Twitter followers and arse lickers in your organisation don't mean you are authentic.

You're a chancer. You know it, I know it and plenty of others know it too.

What's your other classic – "don't see pound signs over other people's heads". Is that why you tweet to the likes of Theo Paphitis? ❞

Just be aware that as you and your business become more successful and your profile in your field increases, you may become a target for jealous nut-jobs. So many people are waiting for me to fall over – sorry, you'll have to continue to wait.

Otis Ogle (*www.ipsx.co.uk*) said to me,

❝ I've heard many a story like this – somebody in the gutter, struggling, works stupidly hard, succeeds, starts to spend money and boom, people are suddenly up in your face asking you WTF you're doing. 'Erm, I've just spent 6 years working my arse off, I'm now buying my mum a cottage, so get out of my face please mate...' These are the kind of people that would key your car. ❞

Car-keyers, I like that, I'm having that one. "Car-keyers" is this season's *GOYA* phrase, following on from "cufflinkers". Who the hell would key a car? It's nasty, but every day there are people who set out to ruin other people's things just because they don't have them.

I call myself a "Marketing Genius", total irony, although maybe I am, because the line on the front cover of *GOYA* says, "Voted best business book of 2009", with, in small text, "By my mum".

I've since seen "Best business book of 2009" quoted on loads of reviews, with the little rider conveniently missing, hilarious!

I did that because when we launched *GOYA* we had no reviews, nothing, no collateral, no 'front cover quote', so I just made one up!

Funnily enough, when organising a reprint, my editor suggested we lift a quote from any of the 100+ average 4.9\5.0 Amazon reviews and put this on the cover.

I thought about it but in fact decided that I wasn't going to get a better quote than "*Voted best business book of 2009"!

At times you may find yourself in the same boat, not having something you need for your business. Actually most times the only thing you really need is shoe leather, a phone and a willingness and ability to make things happen with what you HAVE got.

As you will know by now, I surround myself with some exceptionally smart operators who actively look out for me. In football there is no point in having a team just made up of David Beckhams. You need midfielders, defenders, a goalie and a coach and that also applies in business: you need to have a rounded team with a balance of skills.

Something which has really helped us is having an amazing Public Relations team in the form of *www.avidpr.co.uk*. I met Avid's MD Mira Taylor at a 4Networking launch over in

Manchester and told her that my experience of PR was largely Pointless Rubbish. She kind of agreed and said, "If you're after lengthy activity reports, jog on".

Three days later, rather than sending me a proposal, she rang me and asked me to check out page 6 of *The Times*. Lo and behold, there was my name in print alongside some snooty top business bloke from BT.

No proposals, she just went off and proved that she could deliver results for us.

18 months on, she's still doing that, week in, week out. Just shows that in business sometimes you don't need fancy proposals to win business...

You just need to do what you say you can do!

Anyway, back on track. You need to get people talking about you, ideally positively, but negatively is OK too. In business, you need to be a story teller. People love stories; I know I do.

Having now been to loads of conferences, why do they keep fielding dull speakers waffling shit about hedge fundZzz?

Borrring

Four years ago I was a "fat bumbling idiot" who, by practising, practising, practising, has since become a 'professional speaker'. This has been as a result of doing huge numbers of 'insights not sales pitches' aka 4Sights at 4Networking meets.

These really are a fabulous test-bed. You can refine your message and test the reaction of various different audiences rather than, as was suggested to me, going to a Professional Speakers' Association type gig, where everyone is just *cuff-linking and trying to outdo each other.

That certainly wouldn't have worked for me. I'm too unconventional, I reckon. So in fact this journey for me has been one of self-development, using the network over time to build up my skills and my confidence. This is the same network that I am urging you to seek out. It's not some VIP, exclusive club; it's the same one that is available to everyone.

If I'm honest, I never anticipated any of this. Yeah, maybe 40 4Networking groups or so, but national TV, papers, radio... 300+ groups across the UK with international groups launching in early 2011: how the hell did that happen?

If you hear me on radio, see me on telly, you can be sure of one thing –

If I'm totally honest...

I'm still waiting for someone to find me out!

Me & my
Twitter mate
Theo

http://twitter.com/
TheoPaphitis

CHAPTER 12
Roll the dice

O oh I do like a good metaphor, so here's one for you.

~~~~~~

66 I can still picture the particular snakes and ladders graphics on the version of the game I had as a kid and I'm sure you can with yours too. Why did we love that board game so much?

After all, there really is no skill involved. 99

~~~~~~

Probably because we were 8…

~~~~~~

66 Your fate is governed entirely by the shake of a dice. Land on a good square and you go up, a bad square and you go down. But in fact, as you play it, you experience all sorts of useful emotions.

Over-confidence creeps in as you get two or three ladders in a row, which then makes the next snake seem a bigger blow. There's complacency as you near the top, only to hit that long snake about 4 squares from the end. Petulance and a claim that things are 'unfair', when you hit snake after snake. Ruthless competitiveness creeps in, and also schadenfreude (I love that word), that "mischievous delight in the misfortune of others". It is this, let's face it, which is at the heart of the game. It's a guilty pleasure, but one that really must stay within the confines of the board.

In self-employment, in my opinion, compared with making a living in the corporate world, there are far more rewarding ladders, but, let's face it, there are also deadlier, more unpredictable snakes. So, it's good to know that when the shake of the dice goes against you, that networking provides a great way of helping you get back into the game. **"**

I'd like to take the credit for the above, but it's been lifted directly from a piece on Tamsen Garrie's blog at *www. tamsengarrie.biz*. It was too good not to include, even if I'd never use a word like schadenfreude... I do like it.

Tamsen's blog is a belter, updated regularly with interesting and thought provoking material: do check it out.

We've all played snakes and ladders and, after all, that's what life is. A big Fuck Off game of chance.

If you look at your life now, let's say, in terms of whatever you deem to be "success", what part of the board would you place yourself on?

When I was employed, the square on the board I thought I wanted was a nice 3 bed semi, working for The Man, going to work early, returning home late. This would have been a step up, as at the time we were living in a 2 bedroom terrace and before that a rented council maisonette above a row of shops.

But surely my life had to be more rock n' roll than living above a chippy? No matter what my dream was, it was never going to be realised while someone else, my employer, rolled my dice.

So there comes a point when you need to roll them – maybe the point when you *really* take control is when you are compelled to by frustration and unhappiness with your lot.

If you've read GOYA, you'll know that, two weeks before Christmas 2004, I told my boss to shove his job up his arse and I walked, with no savings or plan… other than a vague idea of starting my own business.

If on that day I'd asked my "supportive" wife to tell me in percentage terms, how happy she was with my decision, she would have said "0 %".

Fast forward six years – I've just asked her how happy she is now that I chose to leave when I did to start my own business and her reply is "100%".

In your life you'll get those moments when things change, when you're no longer happy with your position. I can recall the exact minute when my mind was made up, when I made the decision to go from being employed to self-employed.

I'm repeating myself here from *GOYA*, but it's important.

For me, that exact minute was driving past a bloke who was driving into a big house which even had electric gates. At the time I was working for a firm in London, doing silly hours. I thought to myself, "Sod this, I could work 120 hours a week for them and I'd still never be able to afford the electric gates, let alone the flash car."

Truly, in that instant my mind was made up.

My own Robert the Bruce moment.

Imagine if I'd not left work at the time that I did and had driven down the road five minutes later – who knows whether you'd be reading this book or not?

How many times have you stayed in a relationship or a job much longer than you wanted to?

If you're there now, in a loveless marriage, an abusive relationship, a shitty job or a situation that takes more out of you than it gives, here's a way of giving you the strength to make the call.

Here's what I do, I always ask this question when making tough decisions: imagine two buttons, one marked STAY and one marked GO and you could press either of them and the outcome would be completely UNEMOTIVE and painless, with no stress, no pressure, no emotions, no tears.

Which button would you press?

Whichever one it is, there's your answer.

It's hard to find the energy to break a cycle that isn't working for you. Change is difficult.

But there is a nigh-on perfect life, perfect partner, perfect job and perfect business out there for you.

Really there is, I'm proof of that, but you do need to be brave enough to roll the dice.

And whether you are rolling the dice or not, take it from me, snakes will find their way into your life. Ladders on the other hand, well you are going to have to seek them out.

As for the whole procrastination thing, once people have moved on, more often than not it's because the pain became unbearable and it's always the case that people wish they'd done it a lot earlier.

Having said that, when everyone is telling you to get out of a *shituation*, but you choose to stay in it, it's not because you are weak, but because you are strong. What about the boxer who has a game plan that revolves around taking a load of punishment in order to get into range?

In my case it was starting a marketing business off with no savings, no income and, to be truthful, no real idea other than I was going to make it happen.

This was a big deal for my family, but the wife had nothing to fear – after all, we had a big jar of change to fall back on.

You may have seen the Coinstar machines in your local supermarket. If you've been in the same situation I was in, the likelihood is you've used them!

For readers who don't know what the hell I'm talking about, you bring along a big bag of your old coins and pour them into the machine and it sorts them out. You end up with a printed voucher you can swap for cash, which in my case was £78.13 less 8% commission: £72.35.

Once you've banked your change jars, bang, it's gone. It's a kind of low level liquidation of assets.

I would have been better using the 2ps and 1ps to buy milk and bread each day but the pain (and embarrassment) would have been just too much. This applies to your business: sometimes it's worth paying that 8% for an easy life.

Back then, my one page business plan looked good on paper. The "supportive" wife said, "So does fish and chips".

You may need to roll the dice on behalf of your tribe and that includes hesitant partners. It's really not pleasant having to tell those you love that you've just landed on a big snake.

It's even worse when you've been talking about a life made

up exclusively of ladders.

Remember Sharon Wright, British inventor of the year, the creator of *Magnamole*, who I mentioned a few pages ago? Having the Dragons fighting to invest in her and her business must have felt at the time like the ultimate ladder. Her invention is "The powerful pick-up tool for safely threading wires and cables through cavity walls." Like all great inventions, it's brilliant in its simplicity and when you look at it you wonder how on earth no one had thought of it before.

So, great product, great pitch, great result. However, what followed, as I alluded to in the last chapter, was landing on a big snake.

When she was in the eye of the storm, everyone was telling her to get out, but she realised she needed to stick to her principles and to her idea. Then when the dust settles, maybe everyone else will understand why she fought so hard. She's been through hell, close to suicide a couple of times: you can read all about it in her book *Mother of Invention*. She's now coming out the other side, working her way back up the board, having learned so much. She is battered and bruised but not beaten. Yet guess what, she still rolls 'em.

There are millions of people who every week sit clutching their lottery tickets, seeing them as the only way to climb the ladder. No wonder life's a permanent disappointment, because on Monday they will be going back to jobs they hate, stuck in a rut where they don't want to be.

Sorry to break it to you, you've got one life. Don't waste it.

A question for you:
Is *GOYA Too* any good?
(a)   Thumbs UP/YES

(b)   Thumbs DOWN/NO

That ends today's psychometric test. If you answered (a) you are an optimist, (b) you are a pessimist. Probably.

My point is this: if your thoughts are negative, you are going to find more snakes, if positive, more ladders.

'Lucky' people are optimists.

I can't promise that by rolling the dice you're going to get the double 6 you want, but what I can say with 100% certainty is that unless you go for it and take a chance, you are not going to move on from where you currently are. You are going to need your internal voice to be a positive one. You may have to mute the influence from people around you who have a negative approach to life.

Some people are never happier than when they just missed the bus. Don't be one of them.

Turn the volume of the positive internal chatter right up to 11.

This chapter has been tricky and this has all stemmed from an initial inability to decide what the chapter should be called. At one point it, was going to be called 'Fail Fast', then 'Fail Fast, Move Fast', then 'Snakes and Ladders, Roll the Dice', before finally deciding on:

Roll the dice

The point I'm making is that this book has had many revisions and changes to make it the one you are now reading. There have been a significant amount of false starts, cul-de-sacs and frustrations that have occurred in order to get something that hopefully now works… after a lot of hard graft and still no sign of the publishing cavalry.

That's how life and business is. It's all part of the journey, embrace it.

So when you're struggling, look for inspiration from those around you that you trust.

Even "marketing geniuses" like me run out of motivation,

inspiration and ideas from time to time. You will too. Remember, you are not a Toyota robot working at a car plant, you are a human, so accept that at times you may not be feeling 10 out of 10. It's unrealistic to think that you can all the time, but if you're feeling 5 or above out of 10, go for it. "It" being moving forward, making some progress.

If you're feeling less than that, do something else, because otherwise it'll put a negative slant on your ideas and your work.

Normally, ideas just flow from my head, more than I can sensibly deal with. However, for the last three days I've had a blank headspace. I'm sure you have also had times like this, wondering if your creative mojo has disappeared forever.

Fortunately I've been here many times before and I now realise that this doesn't last forever and that it always passes. Always.

The same goes for the occasional time when I've been presenting on stage and... died.

In the last seven days I've done three speaking gigs around the country, all with different types of audiences. The final one of the week was on a Saturday and was the one where I thought I'd really smash it.

100 plus people from a Chamber of Commerce: I was the after dinner speaker.

I was hurriedly and sketchily introduced to an audience who mostly didn't know who the hell this nutty over-the-top bloke in front of them was or what to expect.

Four minutes in, the moment every speaker dreads: a sea of blank faces...

Don't worry Brad, only another six minutes to go.

I died.

It happens...it sucks, it's horrible, but it's also great learning too.

What's bizarre is that I used some of the same gags I'd used in previous gigs that week which had audiences falling over themselves laughing.

Not this time... just that sea of blank faces staring back at me... Ugh.

I've now sussed what things went wrong.

1) It was a black tie do, so they asked me to wear a suit, which I did. Now, jeans and t-shirt is my normal thing, part of my brand, so this was a bit like telling Keith Harris that he can't use Orville in his act. From the start, it wasn't 'me' up there.

2) No one knew who the hell the nutcase 'motivational speaker' standing in front of them with a pizza box under his arm was. There had been no publicity prior to the event to explain who I was.

3) The AV equipment sucked: a constantly crackling microphone plus a sporadic and ear-bleedingly loud feedback noise every couple of minutes didn't help.

4) The slot changed from 20 minutes speaking time to 10 at the last minute.

When approached about the gig, I should have said NO from the start. This is what happens when you try putting a round peg into a *squares* hole.

The point is, occasionally you need to be brave enough to say NO to jobs which are going to create problems. Coming from someone who has previously spoken about talking yourself into things, not out of them, this may seem like a contradiction. But you need to see the ones where 'failing fast' is the correct thing to do.

Even though I knew this square on the board had a dodgy-looking snake with a forked tongue (and cufflinks, if snakes could wear cufflinks) lurking on it, I went for it all the same.

If you discover you've made a bad decision, as I had, the

best thing to do is what I did – as soon as I had finished and had received my polite golf clap, I got the hell out of there.

Get failure out the way quickly, learn and then move on.

Gordon Brown, who I said in GOYA would be a great Robin to someone's Batman

turned out to be more a *robbin' bastard*, now that we've been able to see the state of the country's coffers i.e. empty.

He didn't fail fast, he failed slow, and created huge problems as a result of his slow demise. Spending budgets have just been slashed.

And the "nation's favourite", Business Link, has been scrapped.

KPI city. Business Link was a very cosy, comfortable ladder for those who worked there and of course now that it's turned into a snake, people are trying to slide down it as slowly as possible... that way they keep getting paid and perpetuating the myth that they are adding real value to business.

They talk about "signposting groups", *what on earth are they*? Any idea?

All they "signposted" for me in my first month of trading back in 2005 was a frigging £500 professional indemnity insurance certificate that I didn't want or need.

At the time I'd never even had £500 worth of sales.

What a joke.

It saddens me because when I started out I knew no better. I looked to these guys for advice: after all, the "Government was funding it", so it must be right.

Look, I do know of businesses that have received sound advice and support from Business Link. But the world has moved on when it comes to ways of finding good advice. By smart use of Google searches and places like the 4Networking forum, good quality free advice is just a click (or maybe two) away.

And good riddance to the culture of 'matched funding', otherwise known as double-priced websites and double-priced training courses.

Business Link's own website, *www.businesslink.gov.uk* cost a staggering £35M to set up – that's the equivalent of £2.50 per visitor to the website. Who put up the 'matched funding' for that?? Yup, you and me, the taxpayer. Crazy stuff...

Business Link (and all the other business quangos) seem to have existed just so that some trade and industry minister could stand up in parliament and say that they are spending millions a year supporting small businesses. And yet, talking to many small businesses who are members of 4Networking, none of these organisations seems to have reached out and provided practical, tangible help on the ground. The bureaucracy surrounding schemes to participate in 'tendering opportunities' seems to defeat all but those who are battle-hardened and who have found a way to play the system. From where I'm standing, using those millions to reduce NI contributions for small businesses would have been at least some tangible help that reached everyone. Still, I guess that most of the money has now disappeared from the pot altogether.

The acronym soup continues, with RDAs being replaced by

LEPs ZZz. Let's see if the promise of more local, approachable, accountable agencies produces any better results for the average SME.

Of course there are some good Business Link advisors – I've met some great ones on my travels. But unfortunately these seem to be the exception rather than the rule.

Still, the revolution has arrived. The conditions now exist where it is possible to create independence through interdependence. It's time to rely on the team you build around you, your own network, rather than turning to old outmoded institutions.

Advice and support? Find it through networking groups and online forums you can trust, not (expensive) government agency websites.

Financial support/investment?

Do you really need it?

Remember, when I started my first business I had £25k of personal debt and NO income. Sometimes you don't need financial support, you just need to adapt and change your business or approach. Too much money makes businesses lazy and stupid: get resourceful with what you do have.

It's amazing what alternative lines of credit and more flexible approaches are available if you just dig about a bit. And I'm not talking about dodgy loan sharks...

It's not all doom and gloom! You have the business world at your feet – where you go and what you do is down to you. How exciting! However, if you do find yourself thinking negatively or in a head place which, as our Tamsen occasionally says to me, is "not helpful", you need to break the cycle.

/reaches for bottle of icy water

In the last book, I talked about pouring ice cold water over your head to break a cycle. Judging by feedback, I'm not the only one who found that this works.

So I'll share with you another one of my outlandish ideas which may work for you in helping to move you on.

When I was a kid we used to go through the toys in the mail order catalogue "diggsying" what single thing on each page we would like. As I reached puberty I tended to play the same game with the women's underwear section of the Grattan's catalogue.

/*claps* BACK IN THE ROOM

Anyway, I want you to imagine that you have £1000 to blow on something purely for yourself, not for your business. This is just for you, so what would you spend it on?

This exercise really helps shake things up, as mental window shopping helps to change things.

Just because I have a Jamie Oliver cookbook, the ingredients and follow his instructions to the letter doesn't make me Jamie Oliver.

My food won't taste as good as his, why is that? Because I am missing something called experience. Experience comes over time and through rolling the dice. In fact you learn more in the way of experience through landing on snakes, through mistakes, through adversity.

Oxford based accountant Graham Smith, *www.gsbs.co.uk*, has this to say:

66 I am sat here at the moment with dice in hand as an opportunity has presented itself. Being a planner I am putting together the dreaded spreadsheet. But in the end any number that I put into that spreadsheet is entirely made up. In the end there is no guarantee of success. However, I will be able to stack the odds in my favour if when I make the decision to go ahead, I do it with conviction. If I over-analyse, I might not take the risks that are needed to succeed.

Brad, please don't stop me doing the spreadsheets, they are like a comfort blanket for me. 99

An accountant with a sense of humour, this book really does have it all. Don't worry Graham, your spreadsheets are safe, because I accept that you need to play within your own rule book and use your own ingredients.

What I've set out to do with this book and with the *GOYA* ethos is give you a loose framework in which to head towards taking action. It's then down to you to fill in the gaps and do what works for you.

Whether you choose to move or not, snakes will come and find you... but to find the ladders and the double sixes in life, you must give the dice a roll.

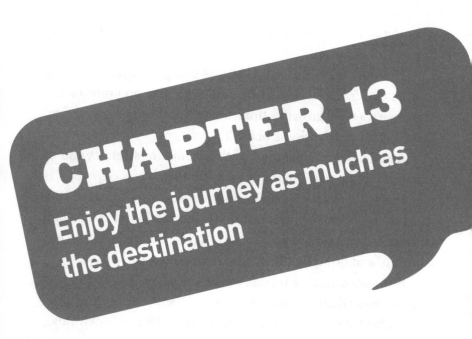

CHAPTER 13
Enjoy the journey as much as the destination

S o I'm laid on my stomach, the smoke rising from the red hot barrel of my tripod mounted sub machine gun and I've still got loads of 7.62 rounds left on my belt feed from the metal ammo box.

The problem is there is no longer anyone to shoot:

every target on my list has been taken out.

For the record, that's a metaphor by the way; I've seen enough armed police in my street for one lifetime thanks.

See, as the network has grown my role within it has changed, it's had to. Initially, like most people, I resisted this change, not intentionally but just because change can be difficult. It requires stepping out of our comfort zone and also trusting that things happen for a reason.

Then my wifey sussed what was going on: I was suffering from 'stage fright'. I wasn't dealing with the pressure of the immense speed of growth – think about a scuba diver ascending, I was getting the 'business bends'!

As a leader, people tend to think you are strong, without fear, but on that particular day I was neither.

I get embarrassed when I'm introduced as the 'founder' - the word sucks, sounds a bit too cufflinky for my liking. 'Managing Director' gives me more of a sense of pride, but my MD role has naturally and quite rightly evolved from those early days.

Business owners who don't want to change stay in the past and then so do their companies. That's why some businesses grow while others stay where they are and then in fact go backwards.

Nick Hill, *www.mrpresenter.co.uk*, said,

❝ How many times do you upgrade your phone, computer, car, office furniture? People look for new external stuff all the time. But it makes no odds to the caller whether you are receiving a call on a Nokia 3310 or an iPhone 4. Don't forget the most important thing to upgrade when the option comes around: Yourself! ❞

Enjoy the fight, enjoy the struggle,

because one day it may no longer be a fight or a struggle and, if you are anything like me, perversely you will miss it and have to seek out new challenges.

4N was built on a war – it was a battle with other well-established business networks. It was a battle over cultures and formats: it became cufflinks v. rolled up sleeves. I'm a bit of a hawk so I quite like a punch-up, but in fact diplomacy has won through and that war is over.

But it's a war that needed to happen in order to allow for a change in dominance.

The war effort of the past has now been decommissioned and that energy and resource has been redirected into building processes and structures to create a network that is both ground-breaking and sustainable.

The war between Coke and Pepsi never hurt anyone.

The true challenge is not to fight for networking market share, but to expand the total networking marketplace. We (and other networking organisations) need to find ways to draw in a larger number of SMEs into business networking right across the UK. I firmly believe that there isn't a single business in the UK that wouldn't benefit from using networking as a key part of their business strategy.

What I've done of late is go for 'low hanging fruit', open goals, sitters. And you can do the same with your business.

Twist. Basket. Twist. Basket. Twist. Basket. Next tree. With limited resources and the need for cashflow, you need quick wins. If your rivals want to spend time and energy going for the apples on the tops of the trees, let them crack on with the complicated, convoluted sales pipelines, weighty proposals and 90 day accounts with local government.

Watch out though for low hanging fruit that turns out to be poisoned. Someone I helped out took a three days a week contract. Lovely, regular money, secure bit of work, no more pressure to pull in work, no worries, but the crucial advice of mine they disregarded was to keep marketing, keep up the networking activity during this time…

They didn't and 2 months later… the contract ended. Back to square one, in the shit. In fact worse than square one, as the momentum building from regular networking had been lost, some bridges already burned.

You know what I've always wanted? It's just a daft whim, but we've all got an indulgence we dream of owning. For me it's always been a full size arcade machine. You can get them, they're called MAME, Multiple Arcade Machine Emulators. Check out the whole mad MAME world on the net, *www.mameworld.info* is a good example. The one I priced up, a fantastic top of the range machine was about £3k, stupid, obscene money… Even more so when I worked out that I used to live on £2800 a year when I was on the dole.

I spoke to my friend Jay (see final chapter of *GOYA*) about it and he told me not to do it. I asked why, and he said,

---

66 I felt the same when I bought my big house – I bought a full size snooker table for my games room and, you know what, I've played on it half a dozen times.

I've got a grand piano in my lounge, which I've played just a handful of times. If you bought your arcade machine, guess what, you'd play on it a few times, your lads wouldn't play on it as the graphics are rubbish compared to your *PlayStation 3* and then it would sit in the corner of your bedroom gathering dust, before turning into *the world's most expensive coat hanger.* 99

Jay was right – the arcade machine was instantly off my menu, as in instantly that he reframed it. I'm no longer buying *the world's most expensive coat hanger.*

Have a think about the material things in life you want and why.

Read that line above again… and again… and again.

The truth is, I wanted and recently bought my dream car, a Range Rover *Sport* (a used one mind you, I'm not that flush/ flash). Ever since I clapped eyes on a blinged-up one in 2005, I knew I wanted one… yet I never thought I'd own one.

But back to the arcade machine – do I really enjoy playing the Namco 1981 classic *Pac-Man* that much?

Nope! I got it on my *iPhone* and played it once. I gave this some real thought, and I sussed out what the arcade machine was about for me. It was about reliving my youth, those innocent seaside holidays in Rhyl when life was so easy.

It was about being a 10 year-old again, staying up late 'til 11pm, eating cheese and onion crisps and drinking Coke through a straw.

Think about the things you want, why do you want them? What is it that they will give you that you don't have now? We all like nice stuff, but look again at what it is you are chasing and why.

Jay had a full size snooker table, which he played on half a dozen times, a sit-on lawnmower he can't be bothered using on a lawn no one else sees.

Are you sure you're not just wanting these things as an affirmation of success to everyone else?

None of it is actually that important, although it's easy to say that once the pressure of paying the mortgage every 28 days has abated. But hopefully this gets you pondering about all the material things that you think you want, because if it wasn't for my mate, Jay, I would indeed have that overpriced illuminated arcade machine/coatstand.

So think about all the stuff you want in your life and then about a day in the future when you've got it all. Then what?

That's where I am right now – my motivation throughout all this has been to make a difference, a positive difference, put my own stamp on this world, because one day, it's going to be all about your legacy, all about those you love.

So tell your friends and family that you love them and enjoy those hugs, because that is the 'stuff' that life is really about.

If you have someone in your life that is no longer around, wouldn't you give a week's wages to once again be able to hold them, to talk to them? Of course, but you live with their memory, their words, their teachings and that's almost enough.

So don't wait to say those things you want to say. Say them now and give that wife/hubby/partner/kids of yours a great big hug and a kiss right now – go on, Get Off Your Arse and let them know just how important they are to you.

Give a friend a call: whoever you are thinking of right now is likely the someone who has been there for you and will continue to be so. Those sorts of people are your rocks, who you will need to turn to as you build your business.

Speaking with Mira Taylor from Avid PR, she told me that during her first year in business she was in fact a bit bored... well, not exactly bored, just a bit directionless: nice house in Manchester, hubby, and two Dalmatians. She now has a business that has totally smashed her initial first year aspirations and targets.

Now what?

Erm…

It happens.

I've said it before, set yourself 2 goals, a realistic one and another where people laugh at you or say "you must be mad."

My friend, Roy Hurley, shared some sage advice about all this. He told me this when I first started in biz, back in 2004:

❝ You know when you are struggling and the washing machine is playing up? You have no option other than to get it fixed up the best way you can and struggle on. You save, save and save until a few months down the line you can buy a new one, but an entry level one. Then when you make it, the washing machine starts playing up again, so you nip out at the first sign of a problem and buy a top of the range one without so much as thinking twice.

Each time you lose a little piece of yourself. ❞

I remember in December 2006, I went with the family for a three day break to EuroDisney, staying in one of their hotels. Breakfast was included and honestly we were so skint, I was slipping breakfast supplies, pains au chocolate and bagels into a plastic gym bag which would be 'lunch': it felt like a scene from *Escape from Colditz*. Exciting stuff.

My weekends used to be so rock and roll, partying hard, but now it's feeling 1000 ply curtain fabric at John Lewis and making decisions about scatter cushions.

Wood-burnered right up!

This is the first time in my 37 years on this earth where I've been not been skint, the first time where I have a bank account that's going up.

Here's my 6 years of business compacted into 1 line:

Skint – Skint – Skint – Skint – Payday – Skint – Skint – Skint – Payday – Payday – Payday

This isn't about bragging by stealth, nor "ain't I clever?" - this is about sharing with you the journey I've been on in my life, of constant struggle, of sporadic self-doubt, which has no doubt got parallels with your life. It's about having finally stepped into a world that for so long I'd looked at, akin to a Victorian street urchin staring longingly at a cake in a baker's window, only to get a clip around the ear from a Peeler.

Mike Morrison, *www.mimomedia.co.uk*, is back:

66 When I hit a brick wall 4/5 years ago I completely shut down – stopped looking after myself, tried to pretend life wasn't happening around me. I filled my days with distractions just to avoid facing up to the situation I'd gotten myself in. Without doubt this was the lowest point in my life.

However, during that time, as a distraction, I threw myself into what had previously been a casual hobby of web development. Those 2 years I was 'under' were when I honed the skills which eventually got me to where I am now. Had I not turned out the lights I'd still be hurtling blindly along a career (and life) path I didn't want, and all this web nonsense would still be an occasional hobby. 99

Just understand this: enjoy and savour the challenges you are going through right now. I mean it – take strength from your courage, your tenacity, your ability to bounce back, to keep on going. It will work out.

A 4Networker and friend of mine, Sarah 'Pash' Howells, ran a business called the Passionate PA. Amazing fun and one of the most beautiful women I've ever had the good fortune to be able to call a friend. 5 foot 11. The world slowed down for men when she walked by. They wilted at her beauty, wit, zest for life and women did too, she was that hot!

And then in June 2009 she called me and said, "I've got breast cancer."

Two days later I drove to Bournemouth where she lived and loved. We ate Thai, got drunk big time... big time...

Trays upon trays of silly drinks, culminating in falling over drunk and she said, "I'll get my tit lopped off, that'll sort it."

That's my girl.

She couldn't make our 4N Christmas do in '09 because she had her operation the day before.

She kept a blog during this period, which she called PMApash, *http://pmapash.org/*, which stood for Positive Mental Attitude, a phrase that in her case was so right. In many places, the blog was laced with incredible humour. Here's a typical extract:

> ❝ I have also decided to rename my cancer Mr Frodo – to be said with a bumpkin accent, please. Mr Frodo is a character from Bored (Lord) of the Rings... a stupid little annoying thing which did nothing but move around and irritate me with no obvious advantage to me, it or life in general. Seems apt. ❞

Pash didn't just write about her situation; typical of her, she went out and did things. In October 2009, during chemotherapy, Pash organised The Pash Bash, a cancer charity extravaganza which raised over £6000 for her chosen charity, *www.tenovus.org*. That was the last time I saw her.

Then on Boxing Day she called me up, upset, saying that the mastectomy hadn't worked, the cancer had spread to her brain and was now terminal, it was only a matter of time.

"How long have you got?"

"Up to 5 years"

I had nothing positive to say. Think about that, Mr Motivator me, I find positive in every situation, apart from this.

There was nothing positive I could say. Nothing.

We both just cried.

On the day Pash died, just 3 months later, in March 2010, she was determined to not let cancer kill her, and it didn't. It was pneumonia and her final words to the doctor were "Fuck off".

That's my girl: The people's Pash is no longer with us, died at 34 years young, as a result of ~~breast cancer~~ pneumonia.

Fuck off Mr Frodo indeed.

Cancer sucks.

We've all been touched by the illness. I also lost my father-in-law, Ray Bennett, the year before Pash died.

Anyway, hundreds of people attended her funeral, including me, with 4Networkers travelling from all around the UK to attend.

She's gone, but not forgotten, and never will be. Every time I hear *Summer of '69* by Bryan Adams, I think of her at her best, at her hottest, at our 4Networking Christmas do back in 2008, doing her Pash thing, using her leg as a faux guitar, see the video here: *http://bit.ly/4NXmasPash*.

That's what this life is really about: it's more about those *Summer of '69* memories than it is about 60 inch tellies.

So, take stock and cherish your own *Summer of '69* moments with those you love.

Live your life like it's your last day, say the things you ought to, to the people you want to – do it TODAY. And for God's sake, enjoy the journey, even if at times it's a struggle, because it's the journey that's the real fun and exciting part, not the destination.

By all means save for a rainy day, but if you can afford it, take that holiday NOW, buy that handbag NOW. Heather Noble, *www.saltsolutions.co.uk*, said, "Today *is* the rainy day", but avoid the must-have arcade machine-style purchases that you will regret about 10 minutes after you've bought them.

Don't be on your deathbed thinking, "I wish I had lit that candle I was saving."

Joy and pain, sunshine and rain, that's how life is.

Tell someone you love them today. It really does make a difference, to them, to you, to your journey.

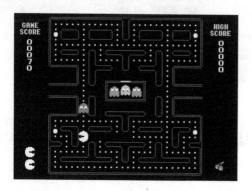

Sambuca qualifies as a silly drink

CHAPTER 14
Get Off Your Arse Too

We've nearly reached the end of the book, your destination is ahead. I hope you've enjoyed this second journey that we've shared together and are thinking, actually this has been much better than I thought!

Since *GOYA* came out, I've received so many emails from people who read the book and then decided to leave a relationship that was going nowhere or told their employer to shove their job up their arse and have gone on to start their own business.

That's a hell of a responsibility to have laid on a book written by a fat bloke from Manchester who doesn't have a qualification to his name, who has been right in the middle of a heavyweight shit-storm, who has spent 4 years on the dole and probably as many years dabbling with recreational drugs, mixing with the wrong crowd, and who on paper was a complete no-hoper.

So what changed?

For me, it's all been about making fundamental changes, both to my life and to my approach. The conclusion to this book is similar to the first: NOTHING IS GOING TO CHANGE UNTIL YOU DO.

We considered putting *GOYA* out just as an e-book, the publishing equivalent of straight to video. Looking at the 100+ positive reviews on Amazon I'm glad we didn't, glossing over the fact that the robbing bastards want 60% of all sales value.

Then I realised that actually it isn't really about the money, it's about the message and that having it in book form adds gravitas and credibility to it. There will be times in your journey when you will get frustrated that people are not listening to what you are saying – perhaps the only thing that needs to change is the packaging.

I don't know if there will be a *GOYA3* or not, but what I can say with absolute certainty is that, if followed, the principles in these two books do work, independently or together. As Tim Johnson says in his foreword, this book shows the 'why' and the 'way' of *GOYA*, with *GOYA1* showing the 'what' and the 'how' to do it.

The biggest underlying principles throughout are that you have to Get Off Your Arse, that good luck fairies are few and far between, and that if you don't start rubbing lamps, you'll never get a genie.

I've shared with you the most significant highs and lows of my life.

Now think about the best day of *your* life and then the worst one.

You'll find that these two significant dates, these bookends to your life, have shaped the person who you are, the life you are leading and are helping to steer you along the path you now walk.

A mate of mine, Mark Crump, Umbrella Corp, shared with me an apt story:

❝ There is an ancient Chinese story of a farmer who used an old horse to till his fields. One day, the horse escaped into the hills and when the farmer's neighbours sympathised with the old man over his bad luck, the farmer replied, 'Bad luck? Good luck? Who knows?'

A week later, the horse returned with a herd of horses from the hills and this time the neighbours congratulated the farmer on his good luck. His reply was, 'Good luck? Bad luck? Who knows?'

Then, when the farmer's son was attempting to tame one of the wild horses, he fell off its back and broke his leg. Everyone thought this very bad luck. Not the farmer, whose only reaction was, 'Bad luck? Good luck? Who knows?'

Some weeks later, an army marched into the village and conscripted every able-bodied youth they found there. When they saw the farmer's son with his broken leg, they let him off. Now was that good luck or bad luck?

Who knows? ❞

That story makes me smile. The traumas I went through as a young man have made me the more resilient, straight-talking, no-worries, fight-for-the-underdog, middle-aged guy that I have become.

I remember, as a 7 year-old school kid, waiting outside the headmaster's office over some now long forgotten misdemeanour. A letter from the school was all set to be winging its way to my mum, which was bad enough, when the deputy head, Mr.

Dixon, came around the corner and shouted, "BURTON! ARE YOU HOLDING THAT WALL UP??"

I jumped out of my skin. At the time, that felt like the absolute worst day of my life, one that I'd never recover from. Fast forward 30-odd years and that now feels laughable.

But when times are tough and you can't seem to see a way out, when things are too much to handle, trust me when I say: it WILL pass.

Sometimes just 30 minutes or maybe 30 hours is enough time to get things into perspective. It's easy to get yourself in a tailspin over situations: take a deep breath, take a walk, get a bit of perspective, sleep on it, take a step back. It's like when you look through a blurred telescope - one small turn of the dial and, blam, complete clarity, a solution and a way through whatever is on your plate.

At the time of writing those 33 Chilean miners have just been rescued from the collapsed mine which for two months had been their home. The papers talk of "rebirth" and the like. I watched the footage of each of them reaching the surface; truly amazing to see the families reunited, the hugs, the tears of joy, the kisses and the smiles.

Can you imagine the atmosphere in the mine during the long days before they were discovered at all, thinking about their families and feeling sure that they were going to lose all that, wishing they'd said they loved them more or taken their loved ones on that holiday as promised? Slightly more complicated feelings no doubt on the part of the guy who left far above him a wife and a mistress, wondering if they were about to find out about each other (and they did!)

So, don't wait for a real or threatened tragedy to realise how sweet and precious YOUR life is right NOW.

Dig out your old photos albums, look at the photos, re-live your memories.

Who are you? Why are you the person you have grown up to be? Where did you come from? Look at yourself as a kid – can you see your hopes, aspirations and dreams within those photos?

Here comes the really exciting thing: think about the images that will be captured in photos of your next 20 years, what does your future hold?

It'll show business success, happiness, beach holidays, big cocktails, chasing kids around gardens, love, cuddles, all that good stuff… so go make it happen.

My drive to succeed has been formed from deciding to run away from nothing anymore.

You are going to need allies, so set up a tribe of people that you can trust 100%. Use networking and social media, but only if you put it at the centre of your world – it can't just be a tick box exercise.

You have to support those people you look to for support – as much as you need them, they must need you. Interdependency, another 'Tim Johnson word' for you.

Support, friendship and a willingness to stick with it, to stick with them, even through the bad times. It's not always like *The*

Waltons and remember even *The Cosbys* had the odd dingdong.

Social media strategy or social media chaos theory, either way is good. Just get out and do it and you'll find it's no longer a case of contacts just from around your local table but from around the country... even around the world.

My business and social personas don't run on separate paths and likewise, yours should be on the same track because you are a person before you are a business and people buy people before they buy products and services.

Invest 100% of your time being 100% you.

If you get it right, the answers and support you need when faced with any type of adversity are right there in your pocket. All the travelling companions you need are connected to you via Twitter on your *iPhone* or *BlackBerry*. I travel right around the UK every week and I know this is true. Anything I need in the way of advice and help is normally just 140 characters away...

People first, business second, that's my rule book. Get the people bit right, the leads and business will follow.

Business success and success in life are not the same. If you're happy, truly happy with what you've got, that's success.

But if you have a dream, a 'daft idea', stop thinking about it, stop talking about it and start DOING IT.

You don't see *The A Team*'s Mr T complaining that he's trapped in a barn surrounded by bad guys... Oh no, he grabs a welding torch and creates an armoured vehicle which he drives through the doors firing cabbages at his adversaries.

Probably not the most robust argument in the closing chapter of a motivational book, but don't take life and business too seriously – have fun, smile, laugh and ENJOY it and the challenges it sends your way.

Be like Mr T: be resourceful, think about what you have lying about in the barn 'upstairs' /*taps head* or your background that will help you win through any situation, any plan, any path you want to walk.

Change the game, scare the hell out of your competitors, be an innovator, use new technologies, approaches and business models to transform your industry!

"Well, because in my sector we don't do it like that..."

Why not? If you have a better way of doing it, do it – you don't have to wait for permission.

Just go do it. By the time you wait for permission, someone else will have done it.

For the first time in my life, reality has overtaken my initial vision, which is just weird! So it's now onto innovating other things, as I can never stand still. So you will soon have Make It Happen Mondays, 4Development, Brad Camp and various other 'daft ideas' for people to 'initially' sneer at.

Follow my lead and make a massive success of your life. Remember it was only a few years ago I was hunting down the back of the sofa for 2s and 1s.

What are you going to change, what are you going to do differently, what are you going to do to change your life, your business today, tomorrow, next week?

Hard work alone won't do it – you are going to need innovation, a strong and loyal support team and a deep-rooted and unwavering self-belief to know when to stay the course and know when to fail – fast.

Most of all you need PERSISTENCE and ENERGY to keep off your arse and constantly improve, constantly evolve.

As a great start point for building your team, get onto 4N and get into social media – you'll find you can punch well above your weight and take on bigger competitors by levelling the playing field and skewing things in your favour.

It's all about people, loyalty and the perseverance to stay the course. It's one thing being cautious, but you still have to make a decision. Why wait?

You can't reshuffle the cards you've been dealt in your life, so stop bleating about it and just get on with it.

Yeah, things can always be better, but they can also be worse – if you don't believe me, try sitting on a bacon-slicing machine.

I hope that our *GOYA* movement continues to create a momentum which no one can stop – an *A Team* with a collective mind-set and a strong moral compass which recognises that the stronger our relationships are, the stronger our collective businesses are – it is this that will make us unstoppable.

What makes my story so special is that it's NOT unique - we've all had our unfair share of adversity but it is this adversity and what you are protecting and working for that *makes* things worth fighting for.

Sometimes, just like me, you will have to make it up as you go along but by keeping your eyes and ears open the opportunities will come.

Our journey together doesn't have to end here – please stay

in contact through *http://twitter.com/BradBurton*. It's as simple as being interesting and saying interesting stuff to get followed back. Remember, it's all about engaging, letting me know what you feel, how it has changed your thinking and moved you on. Tell others about *GOYA* or pass on your copy to someone who needs a kick up the arse, and if you do find the time to drop me an Amazon review, I'd appreciate it, I do read them all.

After 6 months in Somerset my oldest lad Donavon is now living back in Manchester with his gran, but the cycle of no contact has now been broken. A brave lad, he now has his dad back in his life, and I have my oldest. He is actually behind in his schooling and he said to me, "What's the point in doing school work when I'm so far behind? Dad, you don't have any qualifications."

I said "I'm 13 years behind with being your dad, does that mean we shouldn't bother?"

Remember – it's never too late to change direction.

When the going gets tough, you'll always find a way, you really will. How do I know this? Because I've yet to come across a self-employed person who has starved to death.

The final thing I'm going to leave you with is this. I'm living proof that you can take control of your destiny, so make a difference to your life and do something positive with it.

Make a difference.

Follow my religion – Bradism.

Help many. Hurt few. Live life.

Oh yeah... I buckled and bought that iPad... Yours smug bastardly, Brad x

187

Acknowledgements

GOYA Too **has been put together using a virtual team, just as I recommend in the book. We've never even had an 'in the room' editorial meeting! See, the team is scattered right across the UK – how's this for spread-out: Kilmarnock, Altrincham, Gateshead, Sheffield, Somerset, yet it works really well. Of course, it helps that I spend my life bombing around the country to 4N meetings…**

The essence for me of a great team is to be able to communicate in a short-hand way and for people to 'get' what I need straightaway. With all of these people, this is true.

Here's the team:

Design: Paul Williams, Extrabold Design, *www.extrabold.biz*

Paul is based up in Scotland, yet we work closely on a whole range of design projects, from all things *GOYA* to most of 4Networking's marketing activities. He has been a massive part of creating the *GOYA* style.

Editor: Mark Beaumont-Thomas, Lexicon Marketing, *www.lexiconmarketing.co.uk*

Mark is my anally retentive editor, checking the detail and dealing with the grammar, while retaining my 'voice' in the book. While Brad's not looking, as this is the last page of the book, quick plug for Mark's other business, *www.profilebuilder.co.uk*, check it out!

PR: Mira Taylor, AvidPR, *www.avidpr.co.uk*

Mira has thrust me into places I only dreamed about a year ago or so, ooh er missus… She finds PR angles for me and *GOYA* (and for 4Networking) that mean we are being noticed right across all UK media.

continued

189

Advice: Gill Bray, Business Hat, *www.businesshat.co.uk*

Gill's years of experience and wise perspective on business and on the *GOYA* journey has been invaluable and has helped me to knock some shape into the original text.

Media services: Mark Bryant, The Media Partnership, *www.mediapartnership.co.uk*

Mark records the audio book versions of the *GOYA* series and has provided me with some great guidance in putting together the best spoken presentation of the books. All *GOYA* audio book products are available at *www.getoffyourarse.biz*.

Jacqui Turner, The Tweeting PA, *jacqui@thetweetingpa.co.uk*, *@BradsPA*, regularly turns 8 second calls from me into coherent plans of action… amazing. Highly recommended, if you're looking for a PA…

The 4Networking team: The 3 other 4N directors – **Tim**, **Terry** and **Tamsen** + the 4NHQ crew – **Gary**, **Nick**, **Di** and **Gaynor**. Without all of this lot, none of this would be possible etc, but it's true! We look out for each other in ways that have deepened and strengthened over the last five years – they really are my Dream Team.

Finally, thanks to all the people who have given feedback via preview readings and to all the 4Ners who have added such great bits of wisdom throughout the book.

To book Brad Burton to speak at your event or to get him to kick some arse in your business –

Visit: *www.bradburton.biz*
       www.4networking.biz
       www.getoffyourarse.biz

Call: *0845 123 4444*

Follow: *http://twitter.com/bradburton*

I promised to say hello to **Katie Millman** *@katiemillman* and to **Dickie Armour** *@dickiearmour*, a couple of good friends and great people. Er, "Hello"…